Thank you & I hope
you enjoy every word!
Sandi B

Blessings to you — read on!
Michelle Cauen

HEALING
OUT LOUD

HEALING OUT LOUD

How to Embrace God's Love When You Don't Like Yourself

SANDI BROWN AND MICHELLE CAULK, PhD, LPC

DEXTERITY
NASHVILLE

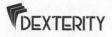

Dexterity, LLC
604 Magnolia Lane
Nashville, TN 37211

Healing Out Loud: How to Embrace God's Love When You Don't Like Yourself

Printed in Canada.

First edition: 2022
10 9 8 7 6 5 4 3 2 1

ISBN: 978-1-947297-33-3 (Hardcover)
ISBN: 978-1-947297-34-0 (E-book)
ISBN: 978-1-947297-35-7 (Audiobook)

Publisher's Cataloging-in-Publication Data
Names: Brown, Sandi, author. | Caulk, Michelle, author.
Title: Healing out loud : how to embrace God's love when you don't like yourself / Sandi Brown and Michelle Caulk, PhD, LPC.
Description: Nashville, TN: Dexterity, 2022.
Identifiers: ISBN: 978-1-947297-33-3 (hardcover) | 978-1-947297-34-0 (e-book) | 978-1-947297-35-7 (audiobook)
Subjects: LCSH Christian women--Conduct of life. | Self-esteem in women--Religious aspects--Christianity. | Self-esteem in women. | BISAC RELIGION / Christian Living / Women's Interests | SELF-HELP / Personal Growth / Self-Esteem
Classification: LCC BJ1610 .B76 2022 | DDC 248.8/43--dc23

Cover and interior design by Charissa Newell at twolineSTUDIO.

DEDICATION

To all those who are on the courageous path
toward healing and wholeness: God sees you,
and He walks behind, beside, and ahead of you.

CONTENTS

HEALING MAP

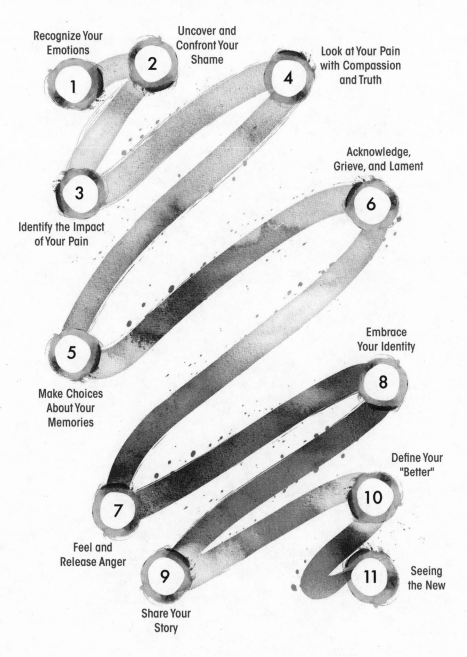

Recognize Your Emotions

Uncover and Confront Your Shame

Look at Your Pain with Compassion and Truth

Acknowledge, Grieve, and Lament

Identify the Impact of Your Pain

Embrace Your Identity

Make Choices About Your Memories

Define Your "Better"

Feel and Release Anger

Seeing the New

Share Your Story

INTRODUCTION

From Sandi:

I had never heard anyone say it before. I certainly didn't want to be the first. But if I was going to get better, I knew I needed to be honest. So I said it, out loud, in the counseling room: "I love God, but I don't like myself."

If that sounds jarring, I understand. That's why I kept my feelings hidden for so long. If the sentiment sounds vaguely familiar, I understand that as well. I know what it is to wrestle with feelings and emotions you didn't choose and you don't understand. Spiritually, intellectually, you know God loves you. (Or you may still be wrestling with the idea that God can love you too.) Either way, deep down inside, you know you have strong negative feelings toward yourself. But you don't know why.

Internally, you struggle. You may say things to yourself that you would never say to anyone else. "You aren't pretty. You're stupid. No one likes you."

You may feel like you can't be yourself—your true self—in relationships. You may feel like part of you needs to stay hidden, way down deep, in the cave of embarrassment and shame.

You may have had some past experience that told you that you weren't valued or loved. Even without noticing, you may have accepted this message as totally true.

You don't want to see yourself through this negative lens, but it almost seems as though it's your default mode. You may notice it spilling over into criticism for others, including the people you love most. It makes no sense when you look at it logically, but it's your frustrating emotional reality. If you have ever felt this way, this book is for you.

I understand the struggle because it has been part of my life for as long as I can remember. And perhaps like you, I remained silent for far too long. One of the reasons for secrecy was that I didn't think anyone would understand. Why was I struggling so much, when in every measurable and visible way, my life was meaningful and successful?

My name is Sandi Brown. (I changed the spelling from "Sandy" to "Sandi" when I was seventeen because I became a Christian and wanted everyone to know I wasn't who I used to be.) God changed the trajectory of my life—and I'm so thankful. I married Mike, my high school sweetheart and best friend. He is steady, strong, and unwavering in his love for me and our family. We have three amazing kids who love God, each other, and Mike and me.

Professionally, I'm the founder and president of the largest Christian radio station in St. Louis, Joy FM, and its sister station, BOOST RADIO. We reach more than five hundred thousand people each week in cities including St. Louis,

Chicago, Minneapolis, Pittsburgh, and Portland. I love my job, talking on the radio, connecting with listeners and Christian artists, and leading a thriving media ministry. I get to see God moving in people's lives every day. Mine included. Because of the growth and my successful track record, I have earned respect and influence in the Christian music industry. In fact, I was the first woman chairperson for the Christian Music Broadcasters board of directors.

I only share all of that information because it helps paint the picture. I recognize the measure of achievement and immense blessing in my life, which is why it was so frustrating to wrestle with this inexplicable inner void. I loved God, my family, and my job. I was also intellectually aware of the love they had for me. But for some unknown reason, I still felt unloved and unlovable—and like a complete failure. I didn't like myself and believed, in my own inner cave, that no one else did either.

How do you say that out loud? I didn't—until 2019. I reached out to someone who had no idea who I was. She was a new counselor to St. Louis and didn't know me from the radio, the industry, or any other Sandi or Sandy. That was important to me. I wanted her to get to know me from the inside out. The confused, unsettled, struggling me who was ready to start healing out loud.

This book is a telling of the yearlong counseling journey with Michelle Caulk. As you read, I hope you hear what is lovingly tucked behind every word. Understanding of the struggle you feel. A desire for you to find freedom. And immense gratitude for the work God continues to do in my life and family.

This book is an unlikely continuation of a relationship that began in Michelle's counseling office. After our counseling relationship ended, an unexpected friendship began. After some time, several discussions with my family, and much prayer, I asked Michelle to help share my healing journey, in hopes that it would offer encouragement and inspiration for you to begin to heal out loud. That is my prayer.

From Michelle:

My name is Michelle Caulk, and God unexpectedly called me to the field of mental health counseling. I was content as a research analyst and librarian before God asked me to join Him in this crazy plan for me: return to school, get a degree in clinical mental health counseling, become licensed, start meeting with clients, and build a private practice. Turns out, God knows more than I do about my own life (no surprise!). The obedience to His voice has produced a really beautiful, really stimulating second stage of my career and calling. It is a career of the heart and mind—and most importantly, the soul. It challenges me each day to show up, to listen, to empathize, and to be human with another human, who is oftentimes hurting and wounded, yet hopeful. I love the work God lets me do every day.

When I first met Sandi, I knew only that she was a woman in the local radio business. I had just returned to the

Midwest following fifteen years of what felt like living abroad (it was Florida). My husband and I were aching to live closer to our families again. So, back we went, and I joined a private practice—where I received a referral for a new client named Sandi. From our first conversation, I sensed there was more to the story. Here was a woman ready to engage in the process of understanding herself better. Of seeing what God had for her in counseling. And of wanting to be seen simply as Sandi.

And so our counseling journey began. It was based in the truth of the Bible, yet also drew on my training as a clinical mental health counselor. We examined her thoughts and looked for evidence for and against. We acknowledged emotions and how they were useful to her—even when she could have done without the painful ones, thank you very much. We incorporated many techniques that may be familiar to you, if you've ever been to counseling: deep breathing and relaxation, cognitive challenging and reframing, grief work, letter writing, journaling, and Accelerated Resolution Therapy. Sandi even took me up on a highly effective treatment called "bibliotherapy," which is reading the same therapeutic book twice!

We applied passages from the Bible to illuminate and clarify the difficult places. We prayed together to ask God to come into the room and provide His healing. We celebrated when God brought her insights, comfort, and peace. After a yearlong journey, Sandi and I agreed that she had made incredible progress, beginning with speaking those painful words out loud and ending with more freedom in her relationships. That voice in her head became much quieter, and her season of counseling with me had naturally ended.

Sandi and I wrote this book out of a heartfelt and empathetic space. Sandi has been there, and so have many women I have met in the counseling office. I'll readily admit that the Thought Monster camps out in my own head, too, at times. This book is a telling of Sandi's journey through counseling and an invitation into your own story—past, present, and future. You may be at the very beginning of your journey, or realizing that you've struggled with these thoughts, emotions, and past painful experiences for years. Sandi and I pray that the telling of this story sparks hope in you. We pray that it helps you know that you are not alone as you wrestle with condemnation and discouragement. We pray that if you see yourself in the struggle, you will also see yourself in the surrender and newfound freedom.

Each chapter starts with a journal entry from Sandi and her reflections on that part of her story. Following the journal entry and Sandi's insights, there is a section called "Unpacking the Process," where I help you apply what you just read to your own life. I have added a few of my personal stories (shame be darned!), as well as those that represent the women I see in the counseling office. This is a reassurance: you are not alone in your struggles, far from it! As you unpack your own story, you may want to check out the additional resources at the end of the book. I have put together a list of books and websites that will aid you on your journey beyond our writings here.

Finally, in the section at the end of every chapter, we have created insightful questions to help you move through places where you may feel stuck. Passages from the Bible and prayers are included to ground you in truth, and you may choose to dive deeper into the Bible and spend time communicating with and hearing from God.

You may have already noticed the Healing Map. As Sandi and I walked through her journey, it became apparent that there were similar "healing points" along the way that I had noticed in other clients. These healing points became places of encouragement that helped Sandi know she was progressing. This Healing Map is intended to show that healing is possible, and that there is a way forward.

Here is a peek down the road at some of the questions we'll be tackling:

- How do you both listen to your past pain and move forward from it?
- What is the core belief you hold about yourself, and how is it feeding your thought life?
- What if you began to see God for who He really is and could accept the full measure of the love He has for you?
- How can you tell others your story—or, as we put it, heal out loud—and draw closer to them in relationship?

That last item was more than Sandi could have imagined during the years of struggle or when she first reached out for counseling. But now she knows it is possible because she has experienced it firsthand. But this is not just to relate Sandi's story. Sandi and I wrote with hope held close: that God will use this book to usher in a similar story of healing in your life.

This time is a chance to process your past painful experiences, thoughts, and feelings—perhaps by yourself, with a couple of friends, or with a counselor—to gently challenge unfair narratives, and to give yourself permission to think and feel differently, harmoniously, and peacefully. Your journey will be unique to you. At times, you may feel overwhelmed and need to take a break. Please do so! At other times, you'll feel hungry for this material and absorb it at light speed. Take it in at a pace that feels most honoring to you and what God has for you.

As you read, Sandi and I hope this becomes more and more about your story and your healing. Grab a pen, a notebook, and some tissues (tears are encouraged in this space!), and do your best to walk through this journey. It will be hard to confront those old messages that you've heard or you've told yourself again and again. But, know you are not alone.

Are you ready to take a very courageous step? A step of discovery into your story?

There is hope, and there is healing. It will take longer to heal than it will take to read this book. That is okay. Give yourself permission and time to own, to change, and to heal.

Give God, the healer, an open invitation to your mind and heart. Our prayer is that God will use this book to serve as a witness to your pain and as a hopeful, truthful guide to your healing.

In grace and peace,

Sandi and Michelle

Chapter 1

WARNING LIGHTS

I went to a bridal shower for my best friend's daughter today. It was a beautiful party. Which is why I felt like I didn't belong there. I felt like Bozo the Clown showing up at the wrong address. The odd one out. I knew it, and everyone else there did as well. I think.

I cried all the way home. Why couldn't I enjoy the party like everyone else? Why can't I be like everyone else? Pretty. Girly. Comfortable in her own skin. Do they look at me and see what I see? If so, why was I invited? If not, why do I feel this way?

I couldn't bring myself to tell anyone how I felt. But I did make a joke about it to my family and coworkers. "I felt like Bozo the Clown at the wedding shower," I said, laughing heartily. They chuckled and said, "That's not true." But I know it is.

For as long as I can remember, that's how long I have felt this way. It's like my mind and heart are out of sync. What if the constant "I don't like me" message could go away, or at least simmer instead of boil? What if the future could be less confusing? What if my emotions could get untangled and I could enjoy being me? What if I could actually

*discover "me" in this process? I know intellectually
and spiritually who I am. But what if my emotions
were in sync with who that is?*

What if I could find peace and rest for my soul?

— *Sandi*

I thought I was the only one who wrestled with this nagging, loud self-doubt. The only one with nonstop negative thoughts swirling in my head, convincing me that I'm not good enough:

> *I don't like my red hair. I don't like my freckles, my big
> feet, or my big laugh. I feel inadequate and inferior as a
> woman, wife, mother, and friend. I don't like anything
> about me. It doesn't matter that I've married the love
> of my life, raised three amazing kids, and found the
> unconditional love of God.*
>
> *I still feel like a failure.*

I didn't know where the thoughts came from. Even worse, I didn't know how to make them leave. I just knew it was an exhausting way to live.

On one hand, I could see the truth. I had a family who loved each other and loved me. A job I loved going to every day. I was the founder and leader of two successful radio stations. A respected influencer in the Christian music radio industry. I recognized all of those as blessings and accomplishments in my life. In every measurable way, my life was everything I ever wanted or prayed for.

But I also heard the internal voices that told me I was unliked, unloved, and unwanted. By everyone. My mind knew it wasn't true, but my heart believed it was. It was a constant tug of war and the loudest voice always won.

That was the tension—that despite the good around me, and no matter how hard I tried, I couldn't make myself happy. Peace and contentment always seemed out of reach. The disconnect was obvious, even to me. A constant undercurrent of negative thoughts and emotions flowed through my mind, mostly directed at myself.

The undercurrent impacted every area of my life. I was very uncomfortable with my appearance. I didn't like being in photos or videos or receiving any kind of accolade. Since I thought so little of myself, I believed everyone else did as well. When a coworker, friend, or acquaintance said something kind or recognized an accomplishment, it didn't stick. I heard them, but I also heard the loud, negative "stickier" voices inside. I don't know why I trusted them more, but I did.

Professionally, I chose a career that didn't require me to be seen. As a radio broadcaster, I could connect with people over the air, but still be unseen and untouchable. It felt safe. One of my college journalism professors encouraged that decision. During my freshman year, she pulled me aside and said, "How many chubby redheaded freckle-faced women do you see on TV? You won't be the first. You should go into radio. Then you won't be judged for what you look like." That was sticky.

I don't know if the self-directed negativity stemmed from

comments from others or from somewhere deep inside of me. Either way, it was very real, a chaotic blend of emotions and conflicting notes. They seemed to be getting louder and louder, but since I hadn't heard anyone else talk about their "internal orchestra," I concluded I was the only one carrying this deafening and daunting burden.

The internal orchestra was loud—but not "out loud." I hadn't shared the struggle with anyone. In fact, I worked really hard at not letting anyone else in. The belief was that as long as my life was working on the outside, all was good. But I knew it wasn't. And the secrecy added to the self-blame. It made me feel like a fake, like I was hiding something.

I tried giving myself pep talks, memorizing scripture, and repenting of the negative feelings. I prayed for healing, because I knew this incongruence (knowing one thing but believing another) was not healthy or God-honoring. How could I both love God and dislike myself?

Nothing worked, and something needed to change. I believed Jesus was the key to both hope and peace of mind. I just didn't know how to get there.

I thought through my potential options for seeking help. My pastor? My husband? My best friend? I was afraid they wouldn't understand. I was afraid our relationship would be forever changed. I was afraid of being known, that if they really knew me, they would draw the same conclusion I had. They wouldn't like me either.

The most logical answer was the one I dreaded most: a

counselor. The thought of allowing someone to peer into my rawest innermost feelings brought intense anxiety and fear. Looking back on it now, the fear seems illogical, but it was loud and convincing at the time. Something inside of me was afraid to be seen or heard. I feared the light of discovery.

Thankfully, there was another voice calling. Reassuring and inviting, God was tenderly, persistently fanning the flame of hope. I knew Him as a loving Father and had 100 percent confidence in His power. I didn't doubt Him. I simply feared the process, the unknown.

Hope and fear clamored for my attention. It occurred to me that neither was going to relent. Both would accompany me regardless of the path I chose, whether I remained silent or sought help. If that was true, why not take a step toward hope?

While I wrestled with what to do and how to do it, God was gracious. I received a very unexpected group email at work from a licensed counselor in our area. He shared that he and the other counselors in his practice were available to our staff as needed. The timing was uncanny—a God-orchestrated invitation.

With a great deal of trepidation, I emailed the counselor back and shared I was interested in talking with a female counselor. He recommended Michelle, a trusted colleague of his, and provided her contact information. Seeing her name and phone number in print made my tummy turn a little. Fear and anticipation spun somersaults in my chest.

The emotions felt familiar. My mind went back to my

childhood and a memory of peering down from the community pool high dive for the first time. I had seen other people jump off. They'd loved it and had repeatedly gone back for more. So, I climbed that tall ladder, stepped across the platform, looked down . . . and panicked. I stood there on that diving board while everyone in the pool below stared up at me and anxiety swirled inside me. Could I jump? I wasn't sure.

As I contemplated contacting Michelle, I felt as though I stood at the pool again, my toes on the edge of the board and my heart racing. The familiar internal orchestra playing in my mind. Only this time I heard chords of excitement and curiosity mingled with the chords of fear and dread. Notes of shame chimed in; I felt exposed, vulnerable, and afraid. I knew I was embarking on a big step, a leap of faith that felt like a free-fall into the unknown. I had already decided that if I was going to reach out for help, I was going to go all in. Jump into the deep end. Touch the bottom before coming up for air. It meant being completely honest, being willing to go deep, and trusting the process God was inviting me into. Yes, it still felt risky to call for help. But so did continuing to live this way. I hoped counseling would make me feel better. I didn't know what better looked like or how it would feel, but I yearned for that possibility.

So, I took a deep breath, whispered a prayer, and picked up the phone.

Seven digits. With each button pressed, my heart beat faster. Thoughts collided in my mind: *What should I say? How do I even put words to what I'm feeling? Will she understand? Will she think I'm crazy? Am I crazy? Will I like her? Will she like me? Will she be able to help?*

My first thought when Michelle answered the phone was, *Hmm. She sounds normal.* (I don't know if Michelle had the same feeling about me.)

"Why do you want to see a counselor?" she asked.

I had rehearsed the telling of my issues beforehand. The goal was to give her an idea of the struggle without sounding like I had lost my mind. I replied, "Something's not right, and I'm at a loss with trying to figure it out. I'm hopeful that you can help. I have so many mixed emotions, and I don't understand why. It seems like my emotions aren't all rooted in truth. What I think and what I feel are sometimes out of sync. And one more thing . . ." Deep breath here. "I don't like myself. And I don't think that is God-honoring, but I don't know how to change it. This feels like a very desperate thing to do—reaching out for help."

I closed my eyes and waited for her response. I waited for the kind of rejection I had been telling myself for years. Instead of ridiculing me or chastising my lack of faith, she graciously said, "Reaching out for help isn't desperate. It is a very courageous thing to do."

And so, our journey began.

Much to my surprise, as we delved into my background during that first call, Michelle was inquisitive and affirming and unfazed by my laundry list of conflicting emotions. In fact, she shared how our emotions are like warning lights on a car. When they beep or flash, it indicates that something is going on that deserves more attention. She continued to explain that God lovingly wired us this way so we could respond to issues before they get out of hand.

Mind blown.

The understanding that my feelings and emotions weren't a problem, but were rather my inner self trying to say something, brought a measure of instant peace. The realization that God had wired me this way brought comfort. And the thought that there was a road of discovery ahead into my issues brought both curiosity and a tinge of fear. What were my emotions or warning lights trying to tell me? How could I discern what they were saying? And what should I do to fix the problem? Those were questions for another day . . . and further into this book. For this moment, though, this big, scary jump into the deep end? It was exhilarating.

I don't remember all of the words spoken between Michelle and me that day. But I remember the key points I heard during our forty-five-minute conversation: understanding, grace, hopefulness.

When the call ended, I felt relieved and a little giddy. With no more somersaults in my tummy, the anxiety meter dialed back a bit. I felt good. Nothing had changed in my overall situation, but it felt as though something was different. I had shared some of my truth, and it was freeing. On one hand it was merely an introductory phone call, but it felt like much more. I had been honest and transparent. I'd allowed someone else, for the first time in my life, to get a glimpse of the real me. And Michelle hadn't cringed, judged, or dismissed me.

It was the first step. A big one. I took a breath and felt a desire to do it again—to jump off the high dive and go deep.

UNPACKING THE PROCESS
WITH DR. MICHELLE

Jumping In

I love what I do for a living because I get to witness these precious, meaningful beginnings in my clients' journeys. That moment they take a breath and step off the diving board. I'm not a lifeguard, but I'm someone who can swim alongside for some time, lending a helping hand, offering encouragement.

When I begin with clients, one of the most critical gifts I can offer them, especially at the early waypoints in their journey, is the confidence of hope. Hopefulness of change. Hopefulness that things will get better. Hopefulness that they will heal. I do this because oftentimes they are not in a place where they can hold onto hope themselves. So, I get to do it for them.

I'd like to offer the same for you, the reader. Before we dive into this journey, before we start to explore the hard stuff, can

I offer to carry some of your hope for you, until you can pick it up again? That's what good counselors, friends sitting around the table, sisters who listen, all inherently do: carry hope when it seems hopeless. Until you are ready to take that precious promise back again.

As a counselor—and as a friend, sister, and daughter—I engage in many conversations like the one I had with Sandi. I know how incredibly difficult they can be to initiate. On the one hand, there are the exterior justifications: I can't deal with this now. Too many chores, too many work deadlines. I haven't even gotten my teeth cleaned in a year, and you want me to spend an hour each week sitting on a couch in front of a total stranger?

Even more persuasive is the internal narrative. That little (or sometimes shouty) voice that nags us: *My friends and family don't have time to listen to me talk about my struggles. They have jobs, kids, and fifty loads of laundry backed up to last month. That's more important than I am.*

And then there's that base fear—the one that deals with confronting ourselves and looking at the past. This is the scariest type of fear there is, this feeling of opening Pandora's box when the lid has been firmly bolted shut. At its heart, there is also the very present fear of losing control and staying in the painful place once it's brought to light. What if talking about it makes it even more real? What if, when I start to talk about all this painful stuff, I just crack wide open and can't put it all back in?

Just as I heard Sandi's underlying apprehension that day,

I know you're probably thinking, *I want to dive into the pool, too, but I can't see the bottom.* Your toes are at the edge of the board, but you're scared. You're worried you'll sink. You're contemplating how not to belly flop into rejection. You're looking around for the kickboard or water wings, but someone else has already claimed them. You know the water runs deep.

I'm here to tell you to jump anyway.

It takes bravery to leap into those still, dark waters and see yourself with the fullness of emotions, shame, and past pain you've kept inside. But doing so means you also recognize and claim the truth that there's more to your story—and beautifully, more to God's story for you.

Ready to jump?

Let's start by talking about emotions. They come first because, well, we experience them first. Like Sandi, you may have had some emotional reaction that is causing you to reach into this book. As women, we are on one hand very in tune with our emotions. Every day we navigate a vast range of feelings— maybe it's irritability at an alarm that has gone off before we were ready to face the day, joy at a baby's laughter, or loneliness when our spouse misses hearing a part of our hearts. And everything in between. Life would be an utterly flat, boring experience without these daily sensations, wouldn't it?

We feel these daily emotions deeply, whether we speak them aloud or not. Emotions, both negative and positive, are a very human part of life. But we often also misunderstand what our emotions may be trying to tell us. We know how we feel, but we don't know how to interpret those feelings and how to integrate them with truth.

This is especially true of critical and negative thoughts, and the result of those harder emotions is that we try to suppress or ignore them. Doubly so for those harder emotions related to past pain. The emotional pain you thought you had kept a carefully tightened lid on. But hiding or suppressing them is not honoring their designed purpose.

Have you ever considered that your emotions are sending you a message? The undercurrent of your negative self-talk is trying to tell you something. And that's a good thing. Just as your car warns when you are low on fuel or a tire is going flat, your internal alert system likewise sounds the alarm. Your emotions are there to tell you when something is off so you can fix it before it becomes a bigger problem.

Let that sink in. You aren't a bad person because your emotions are in conflict. Each one is simply an indicator of something going on beneath the surface. As painful as it might feel at times, it's a normal process.

What are some common warning messages you may feel? They could be:

- Reoccurring thoughts that you're not good enough
- A puzzling sense that something is wrong
- A general dissatisfaction with self and life
- Anxiety, sadness, depression, fearfulness
- Irritability with self and others
- A feeling of disconnect from self and others, including God

Do any of those messages or emotions sound familiar? Does one in particular seem like it has been in alarm mode for a while? Perhaps more than one? Have you ever considered what the underlying message is? What the warning is for or about? What requires attention?

Emotions such as sadness, fear, anger, loathing, resentment, jealousy, regret, and disappointment simply tell us there's some underlying pain or threat that needs to be attended to. Anger, for example, tells us to respond with the fight, flee, or freeze mechanism when there's a threat to our well-being. Sadness lets us know we've lost something precious, and we need to grieve that person or thing that's no longer around. Emotions are normal, valid, useful, and certainly a part of how we live and move in the world.

They are useful as well in indicating that something needs to be attended to, just like warning lights. For example, when anger festers into resentment, it then deepens into bitterness. Anger, while useful at the beginning, can worsen into a kind of emotional cancer that affects relationships, your sense of peace, and even your connection with God. Likewise, when the grief of sadness isn't tended to, it can also deepen to the point of depression. Untended, grief can cause a withdrawal from others, a loss of self-worth, and a cynical view of the world and others.

In the coming chapters, we will dig further into a variety of emotions, including sadness, anger, peace, joy, grief, and more, and how to continue to identify and work through them in a way that responds to your warning lights. Trust me, as a counselor, I am not going to tell you to hurry up and resolve these emotions. We are going to unpack them so you can understand what they are telling you and how you may intentionally, and with a healthy heart, move with and through them. We will examine, too, what God has to say about our emotions.

Here's the good news about these tough emotions: they can be resolved. You don't need to remain stuck within that endless cycle of negativity, fear, or pain. With God's help, you can move forward, releasing those emotions and moving them along so there's more space for all the good stuff in your life.

If that was the good news, here is the challenging truth: oftentimes, we assign "should" or "shame" to our emotions. We beat ourselves up for daring to be less than joyful. We tell ourselves, *I have so many good things in my life, I shouldn't feel this way.* Or, as a follower of Jesus, *I shouldn't still have these negative thoughts.*

Repeat after me: "My emotions are neither good nor bad. They just are." Stop judging yourself for feeling the way you do. You can "should" all over yourself, but it doesn't resolve the issue. All it does is pile more on to the core emotion and keep you from finding peace.

So here we are, warning alarms blaring. We know it. We don't like it. We may feel embarrassed or ashamed—which is why we've tried to ignore the cadence for so long. Think about it: we are built for pain avoidance. It is a survival mechanism. We move toward good and move away from bad. That makes sense if we're dealing with a hot stove, but attempting to ignore, tuck away, or live around emotional pain doesn't work. Time does not heal all wounds.

Emotionally, we try to self-diagnose, self-treat, and sadly, self-medicate. We're used to solving problems, right? We fix things all day, every day. But this (whatever this is) doesn't seem to be fixable. It's too difficult, too big. And our loving heavenly Father hasn't fixed it yet either, which only adds to our frustration.

Whoa. Did I actually just say that?

Yes. Because I've been there too. I've felt that frustration. I've felt unsure as to why God hasn't stepped into this part of my life . . . yet. Maybe you have as well.

Can we pause and remind our hearts of something? God is good. He is perfect. Throughout scripture we see His mercy and compassion on display. He is moved by our pain. He alone is our healer; there is no healing apart from God. He is the only one who can create, recreate, and restore. He is all-sufficient and offers Himself and His love fully.

So, why then, if we love God fully and He loves us fully, are we still struggling emotionally? There is not one simple answer. We live in a broken world. Sin and its consequences are rampant. Pain, as unfair as it feels, is a shared reality on this side of heaven. And sometimes, as we seek to protect ourselves, our unresolved pain and wounds create barriers in our lives—walls that keep us from engaging fully with others, including God. These barriers linger in our hearts and taunt us with untruths. *You can't trust anyone*, they whisper. Or maybe, *You obviously don't love God enough for Him to help you.* Or even, *God doesn't love you enough.* The lies and the pain, over time, become louder than the truth. We carry both, and we're caught in the swirling middle, wondering why God hasn't stepped in and made it all go away.

Consider this: what if God's loving plan for you is more of a journey than a one-and-done emotional fix? What if His plan includes identifying the core warning-light issues that have become barriers around your heart? And what if that kind act reveals His heart toward you? That He not only wants to usher in healing, but He also wants you to discover more of His character and faithfulness in the process? He may even want to reveal truth and comfort that you can share with others. He stands ready to love you through a process that leads to full, honest engagement with Him and others.

This is the journey Sandi and I wish to help you begin. Above all, we hope you will internalize this truth: the fullness of God's love can invade and hush the confusion and pain in your heart. Hold onto that knowledge as we walk forward, together, on this healing journey.

To help with that journey, at the end of each chapter we have included a version of the Healing Map that corresponds to the step toward healing we have just explored. As I mentioned, I created the map after seeing commonalities, or markers, in the counseling process for many of my clients, including Sandi. The map is intended to outline some common markers of progress, as you journey on toward healing and growing in relationship with yourself, others, and God.

As you see progress, you'll be encouraged to continue through the rockiest of terrain and the steepest of hills, map in hand. However, healing is more than just following directions. During each point on the map, consider how God is leading you, where He is asking you to go, and what provisions He is giving you along the way. These markers may resonate with you, or you may discover others that apply better to your unique process. When you see the Healing Map after reading each chapter, pause and reflect, and perhaps jot down a few notes about your progress. You may also find it encouraging to see the next marker on the map as you consider your healing goals.

REFLECTION

God created us as emotional beings, just as He is. Think about the range of emotions He exhibits throughout the Bible. That fact alone should show you that emotions are neither good nor bad—but incredibly purposeful. Even more, our emotions are like those warning lights we mentioned; they tell us something in our internal engines needs to be attended to or else we're going to find ourselves in trouble down the road.

Naming an emotion—developing an emotional language—helps us know what to do with it. Sit in the space of your emotion for a moment.

What are you feeling right now?

_____

_____

Are you permitting yourself to feel the feels? Why or why not?

_____

_____

What are the warning lights trying to tell you? (It's okay if you don't know.)

_____

_____

How can you invite God into these emotions right now?

_____

_____

SCRIPTURE

"And the God of all grace, who called you to his
eternal glory in Christ, after you have suffered a
little while, will himself restore you and make you
strong, firm and steadfast."

— 1 Peter 5:10

"I remain confident of this: I will see the goodness
of the LORD in the land of the living. Wait for the
LORD; be strong and
take heart and wait for the LORD."

— Psalm 27:13–14

"Those who know your name trust in you,
for you, LORD, have never forsaken
those who seek you."

— Psalm 9:10

PRAYER

God, I thank You that You have created me with emotions so I may fully experience the life and world You have created. There are times when I feel like my emotions have the best of me and times when I ignore all of the warning lights. Show me what I am to do with these deep emotions. Fill my heart and mind with Your strength, compassion, and love—for others and for myself. Amen.

HEALING MAP

Recognize Your Emotions

Uncover and Confront Your Shame

1

2

WHAT SHAME?

In counseling today, Michelle introduced the word shame. She suggested it was at the root of a lot of my struggles. Since I've been familiar with my issues a lot longer than she has, I kindly disagreed. I shook my head and told her I didn't struggle with shame. She asked if I knew what shame was. I said, "Shame is what you feel when you've done something wrong. And I know I've done a lot of wrong things in my life, but I don't think I'm carrying around shame."

With a slight grin, she took out a piece of paper and began writing. A few moments later, she handed it to me and asked that I read it before coming back next week. I folded it and put it in my purse. Part of me didn't want to acknowledge it. After I left her office, though, I opened it up and began reading. It was shocking. It felt like I was looking into a mirror. I identified with everything written on the page. I saw myself. And I began to cry.

I thought I was here to learn how to like myself. Now, I have a sinking feeling that the journey forward is going to require me to go back first. Back to where shame was first planted in my heart, there to grow in the darkest places of how I thought of myself.

I want to run and hide. But I've done that for years, and it hasn't helped. My prayer today is a plea: "God, help me stay. Help me look back. Help me walk forward. I trust You."

— Sandi

I didn't realize it at the time, but counseling was an invitation. An open door into discovery. Isn't it ironic that on one hand we know ourselves better than anyone else, but on the other, we often can't see what is right in front (or inside) of us? I reached out to Michelle because I was at a loss. I knew something was wrong, but I had no idea what it was or what to do about it.

It didn't take long for a complete stranger to identify shame as one of my warning lights. I had no idea. Then all of a sudden, hidden pain and shame, tucked deep into the crevasses of my heart, were being invited into the light to explore, understand, and challenge with the truth. If shame hides in the dark, it was time to turn on the light and usher in some honest reflection. Easier said than done, by the way.

Michelle said my visceral reaction to what she wrote about shame meant we were getting somewhere. Little did I know that "getting somewhere," in counselor code, means "you're just scratching the surface." She could have just as easily said, "Buckle up, it's about to get bumpy."

At the center of the page Michelle had handed me, she wrote my name: SANDI. Around my name (like a triangle) she wrote three words: trauma, abuse, abandonment. She explained that I am who God created me to be (at the core), but I have also been shaped by my past experiences. These events cause imprints of shame on my life. Because of our pasts, we learn defenses, cover-ups, and masks that work their way out into behaviors.

Below the "triangle of shame" she jotted down:

- Stuffed feelings
- Perfectionism
- Humor to cover up problems
- Problem-fixing behavior
- Approval seeking
- Feelings of inadequacy
- Drive to perform
- Living constantly on guard
- Waiting for the betrayal that is sure to come

"Does any of that sound familiar?" she asked. I remember thinking, *How does she know me so well? We just met!* Yet she described me with 100 percent accuracy.

While discussing the sheet of paper in her office, I felt exposed and confused. It made me feel a bit uncomfortable. I couldn't sit still. I fidgeted with a tissue in my hand. Moved my feet. Readjusted my position, crossed my legs. Perhaps I kept squirming because it felt like she was hunting, searching for something, and I hoped she couldn't zero in if the target kept moving. I didn't like the words *shame, trauma, abuse, abandonment.* I had never thought of my life in those terms. I didn't like the idea that any of those were part of my past or still having an impact on my life today. I wanted to deny it, but we both knew it was true. I wanted to quit and not talk about it anymore, but I knew that wouldn't help. So instead, I sat there and cried.

Michelle asked why talking about shame caused such a strong reaction. I didn't know the answer. But I said the first thing that came to mind: "Shame sounds awful, and I don't want to admit that it's part of my life. If shame is bad and I am dealing with shame, then we both know what that means. Now you know what I've known all along. That's why I don't like myself."

Her response stunned me. She could have preached to me, reminding me that God loves me and I need to love myself, too, or agreed with me that I was a lost cause (which was a distinct possibility in my mind). Instead she said, "Sandi, what if the conclusions you've drawn about yourself aren't rooted in truth? Wouldn't you want to know? Is it possible that you've latched on to something that isn't true, but you believe it is?"

That got my attention for two reasons. First, I value truth, and the thought that I had believed a lie for so long was unsettling. Second, her strategic question left no space for shame to chime in. It wasn't about what I felt. It was about seeking truth. She was challenging my negative thoughts but was also inviting me into the process. I didn't feel like she was on one side and I was on the other. She invited me into the journey of discovery. And her question lingered with me. Was it possible?

Part of me wanted to believe it was possible, part of me doubted, and part of me was curious. What if she's right? What is shame? Where does it come from? Will it always whisper or shout at me? How can I tell the difference between shame and truth? Have I latched on to the wrong one?

With all of this swirling around in my mind, I said, "Michelle, I guess it is possible that my conclusions about myself aren't truthful. But I'm not convinced you're right. I know what I know." The evidence seemed clear and convincing. Even though my mind knew otherwise, in my heart the verdict had already been rendered: I was worthless.

As I look back at that conversation with Michelle, it was as if she had declared a retrial on my behalf. She wanted me to take an objective look at the evidence. This time, there would be no shameful prosecutor taking the lead. We were going to go back and look at everything with a new lens. It seemed like a tall mountain to climb. The thought of it was overwhelming. And the mere thought of something in my past still wreaking havoc in my life today angered me. I believed I was stronger than that. More resilient. In frustration, I said, "How lame is that? I've got a great life. I never think about my past. I'm mad at myself for letting anything in my past disrupt the good things in my life today. I'm so stupid."

Yes, stupid. That was a pet word of mine that I uttered a lot in counseling. I would never call someone else stupid. Yet it rolled so easily off of my tongue as I described myself. Time and time again. Why is it that we say things to ourselves that we would never say to anyone else? Because shame convinces us of things that aren't true—that's why. And shame was speaking clearly and loudly that day. What I heard from shame was, "You're stupid."

Thankfully, what I heard from Michelle was, "You're carrying both pain and shame. You know one as fact but believe the other to be true. And that's something we can work on."

UNPACKING THE PROCESS
WITH DR. MICHELLE

Speaking Back to Shame

If emotions such as joy, gratitude, peace, and compassion are the flowers of your garden, then shame is the perennial weed stealing nutrients from your beautifully intended life. Shame is more than self-doubt or a low self-esteem or the acknowledgment that you messed up. It fundamentally says to your heart and mind, "I am a bad person." It causes us to want to shrink away, hide, become even smaller than we feel.

Shame is also one of the most misunderstood and neglected emotions we carry. For one thing, we are often unaware of its presence and influence, and that, sadly, allows this unattended weed to grow and flourish in our lives. Even more, when we experience that lightbulb moment with shame, as Sandi did, it creates a powerful and emotional response and may evoke a desire to walk away from the healing process. But it's imperative that we don't. Shame may be one of the most common and destructive emotions we have, and seeing it for what it is—the thorniest of weeds—is key before healing can begin.

What do we need to know about shame to identify it correctly, and how do we know when we're carrying it? Shame tries to—and often succeeds at—hiding in the dark. It not only hides, but it festers and grows over time as well. As it does, it convinces us of things about ourselves that aren't true:

- I'm not pretty.
- I can't be honest about my feelings.
- If they knew the real me, they wouldn't like me.
- I'm not worthy of this friendship.
- I'll never be good enough.
- I don't matter.
- I'm bad.
- There's just something fundamentally broken in me.

Can you hear any of those messages of shame in your head? Perhaps those voices seem louder than God's or louder than the positive ones telling you that you're okay, that you're trying your hardest, that you are still worthy.

Shame is a deeply destructive emotional and relational pest. It's the weapon the enemy of our soul uses to (1) corrupt our relationship with God, ourselves, and one another and (2) prevent us from using the gifts God has given us. Shame can be profoundly rooted in childhood messages, as Sandi eventually began to realize from her own story of abandonment and trauma. Those messages lie deep within our brains and our bodies, and can run quietly underneath the surface until they can't be held in any longer.

No one wants to recognize shame in herself, and that's exactly where the enemy wants to keep you. Here's the hard news: we all have some measure of shame. It's something we've all experienced, from the surface-level (such as that slight embarrassment at tripping over a step) to deep humiliation or rejection (a betrayal by a parent or spouse, for example).

Curt Thompson, in his book titled *The Soul of Shame*, notes that there are two ways that shame manifests itself in our lives:

Hidden Shame

This is the shame you keep to yourself. This can be reflected in the assumption that no one would like you if they knew who you really are. You think, *How could someone else like me when I don't even like me?* All the while, no one knows your daily struggle of hiding behind a mask of seeming perfection. This can cause a distancing in relationships, a result of protecting yourself—and others—from seeing just how bad you are. When Sandi came into the office for one of our first sessions, she said, "I know my husband and kids love me, but I don't feel it." Shame caused a barrier between what she rationally knew (that her family loves her because of their words and actions) and what she could accept as feasible in her heart.

Visible Shame

This one shows up as the critical spirit. Oh boy, *that* one, the one Jesus warned us about when He said, "Do not judge, or you too will be judged" (Matthew 7:1). We react to our shame by turning it outward on others. We might even think we're being critical in the name of accountability, but in reality, we are projecting our own shame in expecting perfection from others. Either way, inwardly or outwardly, we act out our shame. It may show up in the absence of trusted relationships—shame has told us that no one can be trusted, and because of that, our relationships are riddled with feelings of potential abandonment and rejection. Shame may also tell us we're not worthy of love from others, so we shy away from deep connections. The outward signs of shame can manifest in all sorts of coping behaviors: using too much alcohol to quiet that negative voice, or by overworking ourselves in ministry to prove we are worthy to others and God . . . the ways are manifold.

Why is it so hard to admit we might have some shame? As Christians, it's hard to come close to evil. We have—and we should have—a natural adverse reaction to anything associated with the enemy. So, we shy away from acknowledging it. But at the same time, we are living in the darkness of not seeing shame for what it is. Who it is: the soul destroyer, the light stealer, the mask maker.

Doubt, comparison, feeling inadequate, inner anger, or rage leak out. We're unsettled, and we don't know why. We are peace-deprived. Oh, those needy, shameful weeds, sucking the life, joy, and peace right out of our minds and hearts.

Others look at us and see the outward beauty: smiles, family, successes. They see the flowers. They are certainly part of our garden, but we see and feel the weeds creeping underneath, causing us to feel fake. We feel like we can't be honest with others about what lurks below for fear that we'll be viewed as bad people. If others knew about the weeds, wouldn't they reject us? And so, the weeds grow in the dark and the silence.

You may not even know the kinds of weeds in your life. You may simply know that something is off and unsettled. You may feel the effects of being emotionally malnourished. You may feel like you are dangerously close to a tipping point or a blowout. You may feel caught in a loop of indecision or loss of motivation. You may see your life being robbed of joy and your relationships being negatively impacted.

What do you do with all of that?

You are invited to begin to confront shame. Honestly, this is one of the most taxing parts. Confronting shame is hard work. Acknowledging that shame has been whispering (or shouting) in your ear is not easy. Nor is identifying what shame is saying and holding it accountable to the truth of God's love. This is an ongoing process, one that may be wrestled with for years to come as triggers are identified and truth continues to be revealed in the face of convincing lies. In my years of counseling, I've found a pattern that's somewhat unique to shame. It's that many of my clients know (cognitively) that God loves them and that He accepts them, but the heart—oh, the heart!—is a whole other matter. The heart wants to hold on to the shame. It wants to believe the lies because that's what it's done for so very long. And there's safety in believing something, even if it's harmful. It may be what you've always known, until now.

Shame, in this broken world, may always have a voice. It was present in the Garden of Eden when Adam and Eve hid from God, and it still lingers with us today. But we are not without hope or a defense. We can diminish shame's influence by seeing it for what it is: a whisper from the father of lies intended to wound the soul (see John 8:44).

The enemy knows there is power in the spoken word. God used His voice during creation to speak the world into existence. His Word is still alive, active, and powerful as it speaks into our lives (see Hebrews 4:12). On the other side, the enemy uses his voice to condemn, confuse, and shame.

But you, too, have a voice. Are you ready to use it? Are you ready to speak honestly to the Lord, to the enemy, and to yourself? It may feel awkward and unfamiliar. But one of the biggest and bravest steps toward bringing the brain and heart into alignment is to say it out loud: "I feel shame because _____ (insert shameful yuck here)." Don't stop there, however. Continue: "But I choose to believe the truth: I am loved."

If you're sitting in a room by yourself, say it out loud. Declare the emotion. Bring it out into the light of day. Say it to the Lord. He is listening keenly to you, and He desires freedom from the shame that has held you in a place of darkness for so long. It is time!

Psalm 34:5 proclaims, "Those who look to him are radiant; their faces are never covered with shame." You're taking a big step. You're leaning in and inviting God to shine His light into your heart and mind. As you encounter shame, hurt, and lies, you do so with the unconditional love of your Father, who not only reveals truth but has given you a voice to speak truth as well:

Today, I acknowledge that I struggle with shame.

Today, I accept the invitation to confront shame, both visible and hidden.

Today, I choose to believe that I am loved.

Today, I look to the Lord. Because of His light in my life, I am radiant and accept the freedom from shame that He is offering.

Today, I will walk in the truth of discovery and healing.

REFLECTION

Shame has the potential to make us go silent, to be caught in this endless cycle after a painful event. For one, we believe the lie that the hurt or failure defines us, and then second, shame convinces us that we can never recover. On and on until shame is spoken and brought into the light of truth. This chapter has challenged that message and, hopefully, helped you name the shame. In this time of reflection, dig a bit further into the root of your shame, and begin to use the scripture and prayer included below to soothe the shame.

What kind of reaction do you have when you think of shame?

_____

_____

Do you see any evidence of shame at work in your life? How has it affected the thoughts you have about yourself? How has it prevented you from engaging fully in relationships? With yourself? With others? With God?

_____

_____

Can you begin to identify the roots of your feelings of shame? They may come from an early message from a parent, a friend in middle school, or an abusive spouse. You may be able to pinpoint one message or a collection of them that you heard many times. Who did it come from? What message did it send to you that feels covered in shame?

_____

_____

What is one shameful message you can begin to replace with a truth? For example, exchanging "I deserve to be rejected" with "I am acceptable and accepted." It's okay if you don't fully believe it (yet). Identifying it and writing it down are the first steps.

_____

_____

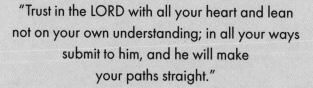

SCRIPTURE

"Trust in the LORD with all your heart and lean not on your own understanding; in all your ways submit to him, and he will make your paths straight."

— PROVERBS 3:5–6

"As Scripture says, 'Anyone who believes in him will never be put to shame.'"

— ROMANS 10:11

"Because the Sovereign LORD helps me, I will not be disgraced. Therefore have I set my face like flint, and I know I will not be put to shame."

— ISAIAH 50:7

PRAYER

God, I confess that I have felt more shame than freedom. More shame than joy. More shame than anything else at times. But, Lord, I ask that You help me out from under the weight of shame. Share Your flintlike strength in the face of lies, and help me resolutely replace them with Your truth, that I am not disgraced because of Your mercy and grace. I know I will not be put to shame because of Your love! Amen.

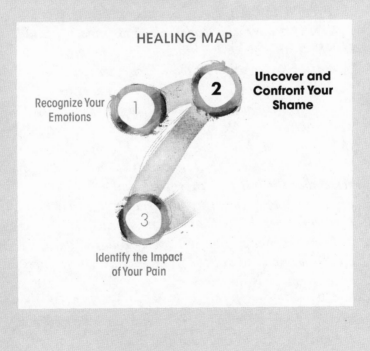

HEALING MAP

Recognize Your Emotions
1

2 Uncover and Confront Your Shame

3
Identify the Impact of Your Pain

Chapter 3

HIDING PLACE

I was five years old the night my dad left our family. My mom and dad were arguing. Loudly. Screaming. My dad said he was leaving and that he wanted to take my brother. My brother didn't want to go with him. My dad left.

That's it. That is my first childhood memory. As I retold and relived the events of the night to Michelle, the details flooded all of my senses. I could see the living room. I could hear my screaming parents. Everything felt loud. Their voices. Their pain. The desperation. The fear. Their words were like weapons. Everyone was getting hit, verbally and emotionally. No one was going to come out of this unscathed. My brother ran to his room.

I don't remember the last words spoken. But I do remember the last two things my dad did: he tried unsuccessfully to convince my brother to go with him. And then he walked out the door.

In my memory, I was hiding behind the chair, crouched low to avoid the flying words, the fullness of pain in the living room.

"Why didn't you run to your bedroom?" Michelle asked. I had never pondered that before. But I knew the answer. I didn't run because I wanted to stay and protect my mom. She was in pain. My heart

*simply broke for her—a five-year-old's version of
the grown-up idea of compassion.*

*Then, it happened. Like unpacking an old box
from the attic and finding something long forgotten
but valuable, something surfaced as we discussed the
painful memory. It made its way into the light.*

In a word, it was unwanted.

- Sandi

As I now reflect on those first counseling sessions, it makes sense. Obviously, I was carrying around a lot of shame. (Well, it was obvious to Michelle, not to me. It's still hard to believe I was unaware of such an influential voice in my life.) But if shame had been speaking to me all these years, where was it coming from? There had to be a root, a "why" that had caused the chain reaction of conflicting emotions swirling inside of me for seemingly forever.

Of course, I had drawn my own conclusions as to why I felt the way I did: I was a person it was okay to ignore, abandon, leave behind. I now know that was a message rooted in shame. But if shame was a resilient weed determined to send poisonous shoots of blame and condemnation into my heart, what was at its core? What was the root? It isn't enough, Michelle explained, to simply acknowledge the struggle with shame. Healing begins when we identify the root message of our shame and recognize it as a distortion of truth.

The discovery journey, for me, started with my first memory, the night my dad left. The invitation was to start unpacking those memories and resulting messages in hopes of discovering the roots of my shame and incongruent thoughts. Since I had kept all of my pain tucked away inside, there had been no one to help me discern truth from distortion or to challenge the negative narrative that I'd told myself over and over. Much of our counseling time was spent re-engaging the past so that I could clearly distinguish pain from shame and understand how to deal with both.

I was giving myself permission to think differently. I was giving Michelle permission to offer new perspective and insight. Here is what I saw: The night my dad left confirmed to my five-year-old heart that he didn't want me. Like my brother, I didn't want to go with my dad. But I did want to be wanted. I wanted him to want me the way he wanted my brother. He didn't. He'd asked my brother to go with him, but he hadn't asked me. I was the unwanted one.

At some deep level, that is what I've felt from that night until today: unwanted. The dots had never connected in my mind before. But now it was obvious, the incongruency glaring: I knew my dad left our family, and I believed I was the unwanted one. I've never known if my dad loved me, but I do know he didn't want me.

I could now see that my feelings of self-hatred had begun with my father's refusal to connect with me emotionally that night and throughout our relationship as I got older. This was the unwanted weed that had spread shame and affected every area of my life.

Truth was surfacing. Clearly. I don't know if I could have expressed it this way when I was five, but a longing to be wanted began in me the night my dad left, a craving and a fear that I wouldn't understand for years to come. I saw what it looked like to be wanted, and I felt what it was to be unwanted. It was a mixed bag of desiring love and fearing rejection. Yes, desire and rejection—those two familiar frenemies have been hanging out in my mind and heart for years. The tension is real. Their voices are loud.

That night also began a longing to be good. There had to be some reason why my dad didn't want me. I concluded that I must be bad or not good enough. I don't think these were conscious thoughts that went through my young mind, but I know with great certainty that they became deep-rooted convictions. I knew they were true because I felt them so deeply. I have silently carried that version of the truth with me for decades.

The root of the incongruent thoughts had emerged. Two conflicting messages. The painful experience of my dad leaving was real. But shame had injected a negative narrative that I believed hook, line, and sinker: I was unwanted. I knew the facts. And I felt the shame. I've carried them both.

My mind went back to the dozens (if not more) of letters I wrote to my mom when I was a little girl. She still has them boxed up and pulls them out occasionally. Each handwritten letter is exactly the same:

Dear Mom,
I love you!
Do you love me?
YES or NO
(please circle one)

39

For years, we've laughed and looked fondly at those letters as a reminder of childhood innocence and our close relationship. But in my session with Michelle, for the first time, I felt like I actually heard the messages tucked inside those letters:

"Mom, I still love you. I hope that makes your heart feel better!"
"Mom, my heart is hurting too."
"I know you love me, Mom. But I still feel unwanted. Can you help my hurting heart?"

Again, I had never recognized it before, but now it became glaringly clear that the incongruent thoughts in my mind have always been present. The letters were proof. I knew that my mom loved me, but I had believed I was unwanted and unloved. And in believing that, I had kept my feelings buried inside, stuffed a layer or two beneath the "good girl" behavior.

More than that, I began to refuse to acknowledge my hurt or feelings. I didn't want to add any more suffering to the family dynamic, so I didn't acknowledge the pain I was carrying. I thought I needed to be the protector of my mom's heart. She was already experiencing such pain and loss. I didn't want to make it worse.

"Did you have compassion for yourself?" Michelle asked. The honest answer was painful to admit: No, I didn't have compassion or empathy for myself. I saw my mom as an innocent victim. I saw myself the way my dad saw me—as undeserving of his love, someone easy to walk out on. I had a fierce sense of duty to protect my mom, the wounded one. But I didn't see myself in the same way. I wasn't worth fighting for.

There was an ambivalence toward myself that I'd never realized before. Michelle described it as being numb or emotionally dead to my own pain. While difficult to hear, it resonated as true. For many of us, this numbness actually functions pretty well initially, as a protective mechanism when pain may be too great. It probably made more sense to try to feel nothing as a little girl rather than acknowledge and absorb the pain of rejection. But the habitual practice of that defense mechanism, over time, trained my mind to believe I was insignificant and that my pain didn't matter.

Can you hear the tension in that scenario? I was emotionally wounded. Unresolved pain was crying out. Shame was chiming in. Both were loud, unwanted voices, so I chose to ignore them. I chose numbness.

Now, in my sessions with Michelle, a new option was being presented. The question before me was, "Am I ready to give myself permission to feel?" I didn't fully know what that meant. I wasn't 100 percent sure I wanted to feel everything. But I wanted to get better. And even though it seemed like a very scary proposition, another high-dive moment for sure, it seemed necessary and potentially helpful to offer myself that permission. I didn't understand why I needed the invitation. But I did. I needed to grant myself permission to change course and acknowledge that my pain was significant. That it had a voice. That it wasn't merely a memory, something linked to a date on the calendar.

The truth is pain deserves to be heard. It has a lot to teach us. Mine had a lot to teach me, but I spent so much time ignoring it, when it demanded to be acknowledged. Pain, as I had discovered in my sessions, is a warning light. It can be ignored for a time but not without consequence.

Even into adulthood, I'd always known I had a broken relationship with my dad. But I hadn't realized the impact of that damaged relationship and how I relate to myself. How I thought about myself. How I talked to myself—the internal dialogue we all have. I had a broken relationship with myself. The negative voices and messages I'd heard so often—for decades—were rooted in my feelings of abandonment and rejection. I simply hadn't known it and hadn't known what to do about it. But for the first time in my life, I was seeing that there were reasons behind all of the self-aimed negativity.

Isn't it ironic? The very voices I'd tried to suppress for decades were the warning lights that God was now using to reveal the path to healing. That clarity alone brought a sense of relief. With this new lens of truth and understanding, I was beginning to see the negative internal chatter for what it was: the voice of unresolved pain and shame.

While I was processing the memory of my dad leaving, Michelle also asked, "Where was God?" I had never even thought about that before. But as we discussed the memory and prayed for clarity, I felt like God opened my eyes to something I hadn't previously seen or considered. I saw five-year-old me scrunched behind the chair, afraid and crying. But I saw that God was there too. His presence. With me. I hadn't been aware of Him back then, but it was so clear now. God wasn't "up there" somewhere, keeping a comfortable distance. He was close. He was with me. It felt like He knew I needed Him, so He wanted to be there. It didn't matter if I realized it or not; He was still there, attending to the "least of them."

I can't explain how powerful an image it was to see God moving in close to my fearful, broken heart. He hadn't left me. He chose to be near me. He wanted to be close. To me! The lie had been that I was unwanted and alone. The truth was almost too powerful to fathom: the God of the universe had come close to me that night. It brought a great deal of comfort and clarity. If God was with me then, He is with me now.

That is true for you as well. God was close every time your heart was breaking, and He is here now. He won't leave. He will stay close as your broken heart begins to heal.

I knew that counseling wasn't a one-game season. We were still in the early stages of processing. There would be more struggles and successes, but this was a good start. The details and memories weren't merely a bundle of pain. In the light, they looked different. I was discerning truth, I was recognizing shame, I was no longer numb, and I was able to feel. Some of the emotion was sad, yes, but some of it was reassuring. It felt like I had tasted a bit of freedom, and I wanted more. I didn't want to hide in the dark, behind a chair, or behind a lie. I wanted every bit of freedom that was available to me.

UNPACKING THE PROCESS
WITH DR. MICHELLE

Connecting Memories

When looking at your personal pain, a key action is to take heart. "Taking heart" has multiple meanings to me. Traditionally, to take heart means to be encouraged, especially when we feel downtrodden or disappointed. The purest form of this encouragement is found in a reference to Jesus in John 16:33: "I have told you these things, so that in me you may have peace. In this world you will have trouble. But *take heart!* I have overcome the world." (The emphasis on "take heart" is mine.)

In my definition, taking heart also means to conduct an intentional survey of your heart. To literally take stock of your own heart and self, and be willing to examine how the painful, broken places and the joyful, free places bump up against one another in your experiences. To take stock is to examine how your emotions, thoughts, and behaviors have formed a pattern out of these experiences. As part of true healing, we must bring important things to the surface where we can look at them. Buried—or accidentally forgotten—occurrences can extend the pain and cause great disruption in other parts of our lives. This is not an easy exercise to complete, but I promise it will help you understand your own story and how the chapters have unfolded and affected you today.

To take a heart survey is to begin the courageous exploration of your earliest turning point memories. These memories can be both positive and painful. This is the moment where you may feel like you want to put this book down slowly and walk away, but tuck your courageous heart under your arm and come on back. When we explore those memories, we begin to make sense of our own emotional, cognitive, and behavioral patterns. Memories aren't just floaty images but rich sources for tangible realizations: "Oh, that's why I do what I do!" Taking the time to explore life experiences may also serve to clarify "muddy memories"—those vague senses that we have but can't quite identify clearly. Through writing and recording these memories, you can begin to understand the overarching themes throughout your life. It's only when we come to an understanding that we can begin to change.

How does one go about an intentional self-survey through memories and life experiences? One of the most helpful writing exercises my clients do is to create a turning points memory timeline. It may take you some time, but it can begin to clarify the root of your pain, feelings, and reactions. It can also reveal how it's brought you to this point. We rarely take the chance to think about the most pivotal milestones in our lives and reflect upon them, and yet it is an incredibly therapeutic process.

Ready to get started with the turning points memory timeline? Pull out a piece of paper and draw a horizontal line smack across the middle of the paper. Use a marker, pencil, crayon, eyeliner—whatever you have on hand. Along the line, you'll write the dates of your memories. Above the line of dates include a few keywords describing the memory, and below quickly write your emotions or thoughts about the memory. Try not to worry about doing this perfectly; the intention is to simply get it out of your head and onto a piece of paper.

For example, on my timeline, I wrote as my first memory: "1979—fell off play rowboat in kindergarten—other kids laughed and no one helped—I was embarrassed and hurt until teacher saw and comforted me." (By the way, I was fine, just a small bump on the head that was an early indicator of a lifetime of incoordination.) You can imagine I felt the same embarrassment and disconnect in writing this memory as I did when it happened. It also helped me understand, as a counselor educator, how to provide a safe space for my students when they feel shame or embarrassment.

On your timeline, you might include memories such as:

- Births and deaths of those close to you
- Beginning or ending of relationships, including friendships, familial, marriage, etc.
- Transitions such as graduations, job changes, relocations
- Illness, injury, accidents
- Personal losses and other difficult memories, such as family conflicts, abuse, divorce

Try not to overthink this exercise. If you find that you

have scant early memories, don't worry. That is normal. Grab any images and feelings you can, and pray to see what God wants to reveal and what He desires to keep hidden. Don't be alarmed if you feel a whole range of emotions. You will also find a combination of both positive and negative memories, and you're encouraged to record both. All contribute to your continued honest examination of your life and growth potential.

You also have full permission to take a break and let it (and yourself!) rest, as needed. Emotionally and mentally, this can be a challenge to complete in one sitting. You may also think about the best way to employ self-care after doing this exercise—be it a walk outside, playing with the dog, or getting a massage. This is hard and good work, and it is okay to follow up with a way to shift focus to self-care afterward.

Once you have taken a break, you will want to revisit the timeline to make your connections between then and now. Keep this timeline tucked into your journal or this book, as you will want to refer back to it during this early process.

As you walk through your timeline, you may find it helpful to ask yourself some of the following questions.

Questions to clarify a memory:

- What happened?
- How old were you?
- Who was present?
- What did you see around you at the time?
- What did you hear?
- How did you feel?

Questions to reflect on the memory:

- For a moment, step outside of the memory. You can be the witness to yourself in the memory, just slightly removed from the situation. How do you feel toward this person you are seeing? Is there space to offer compassion or another feeling toward them? What can you say to them?

- You may have felt helpless back then, particularly as a child or adolescent, when we naturally have the least control over our lives. What does it feel like to see the memory from another viewpoint, from further out and as an adult? How does this help you feel less powerless?

- You may have felt a mix of emotions. It is normal to feel a mingling of the feels when reflecting on memories—and at times, neutral or no feelings at all. What emotional patterns do you see in how you felt back then, and what differences are there now in how you feel, looking back? Differences in emotions can indicate the changes in emotions that can happen naturally over time and the shaping of other experiences in between.

- Can you glimpse God's face and actions in your memories, even in the most difficult ones? How did He protect you or guide you at that time, and how is He doing so right now? Can you see the truth of Matthew 28:20: "And I am with you always, to the very end of the age"?

Now, you may be asking yourself, *Why do I need to do this? Is it really necessary? I want to move forward, not look back. Nothing good will come from it. What if I get overwhelmed and then get stuck in sadness?* Are you having any of those thoughts right now? The unknown can be scary. The known can also evoke fear. It is normal to feel this kind of resistance.

Your pain or wounds may be different from Sandi's. Trauma, abandonment, divorce, loss, disappointment ... Whatever it is, you know it's there. And you worry that turning on the light will only confirm your worst fear: that it is worse than you thought. Or that the pain will never subside. You may feel that as painful as the past was, the worst is yet to come in saying it out loud and facing it. Putting an honest voice to your pain may be scary, but it is also necessary to healing.

From two fellow travelers who have already walked the path, can Sandi and I gently remind you of the good trail that you are on toward healing? Can we encourage you to take a deep breath, say a prayer, and courageously keep going? I get it. I hear from my clients that they are afraid of getting stuck in the feels. That is why so many, like Sandi, tried to avoid them for years. They (and perhaps you) fear that, once exposed and acknowledged, the pain will never diminish or dissipate. The What-If Monster plays out every scenario in your mind that you can imagine. Except one: what if God is faithful?

The next piece to understand in the healing journey is to know that God is present with you. Whether we have felt it or not, God's presence has been unwavering in our lives. Can you take a moment and see Him, woven throughout your story, even when you may not have believed in Him? Can you recognize where He witnessed your pain as it was happening and is continuing to help you through it? (Even as you read this book!)

It may be that you have closed off part of your painful experiences. As Sarah Young writes in *Jesus Calling*: "For a few moments, imagine your life as a house. How many rooms have you invited Me to live in? How many rooms have closed doors? I want to dwell in all of you." Can you acknowledge that Jesus has been there, Jesus is with you now, and Jesus wants to be present in all of your future experiences too? To dwell in all of the rooms means He has filled all the spaces!

God is with you. His presence, His compassion, and His comfort are near. You can move forward. You can look back. You can experience truth, pain, and yes, joy because He is faithfully with you, tending to your heart. As the psalmist said, "You make known to me the path of life; you will fill me with joy in your presence, with eternal pleasures at your right hand" (Psalm 16:11).

REFLECTION

Once you've taken heart and completed your memory time-line, take time to process through the reflection questions below. They will help deepen your learning from your own story and move you toward discovery and healing. Remember, your story is unique, and what God reveals to you through your timeline will be individual as well.

What pattern did you see in the timeline? Did you see a common emotion or thought reaction to these events? How did it help you clarify the roots of your pain?

_____

_____

Hold a painful memory in your mind for a moment. Ask God to reveal His presence to you in the memory or His care for you afterward. How does His presence reassure you in your relationship with Him?

_____

_____

Do you also see where the joyful memories have contributed to who you are and how resilient you are becoming?

_____

_____

"God is our refuge and strength, an ever-present help in trouble."

— PSALM 46:1

"The LORD is close to the brokenhearted and saves those who are crushed in spirit."

— PSALM 34:18

"So do not fear, for I am with you; do not be dismayed, for I am your God. I will strengthen you and help you; I will uphold you with my righteous right hand."

— ISAIAH 41:10

PRAYER

God, please draw the memories forward that You need me to see and understand. Protect me as I go to these places that have wounded me. Help me see Your face in the painful memories and Your delight and presence in the good. You are writing my story with me, chapter by chapter, as I examine my heart, learn from my patterns, and work toward healing from my deeply held wounds. Help me take heart in You!

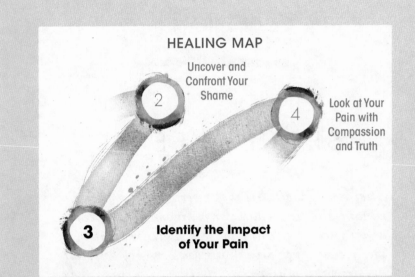

Chapter 4

SECRET KEEPER

After my dad left, life was a struggle. Emotionally. Financially. Especially for my mom. We lived in a government-housing project. I saw my mom sacrifice so much for us. She did her very best, but . . . desperation is a word that comes to mind. I've heard that desperate people do desperate things. I think that's true.

"Do you like him?" my mom asked my brother and me about her boyfriend. We both said, "No." I don't remember if she asked why or if I told her. But I remember why I didn't like him: he was harsh. His words. His actions. Belittling.

When they got married, I was six years old. We moved to a nice house in the suburbs. But to me, it felt just as desperate. My stepfather was always angry. Mean. You could never please him. There was a presence . . . heaviness . . . constantly.

One night, shortly after my stepdad entered the picture, I remember watching TV with him. We were in the living room. I was sitting on his lap. I don't remember what led up to this moment. Was I happy? Was he being nice? Did I want to be on his lap? Did I know what was about to happen?

I know the answer to that last question: no. It was jarring. It was both a rapid-fire and slow-motion mixture of shock, fear, and confusion.

I don't remember what happened afterward either. But I will never forget the moments in between. He was in control. He knew what he was doing. I didn't know what was happening. I didn't like it. I didn't like him. I don't think he liked me either. Why was he acting this way?

I don't remember playing scenarios out in my mind. But I'm sure I did. It must have felt like I had no good options. Tell my mom? And then what? She gets sad. She feels responsible. He gets mad. What will he do? Will he hurt me or my mom? Will we have to move back to the housing project?

Or, tell no one? That had to seem like the best option. I probably knew that telling someone would change everything.

I probably didn't know that telling no one would also change everything.

Confusion. Unfamiliar feelings. Sadness. That night changed me in more ways than I can count. My thoughts. My emotions. My dreams at night. My confidence. My understanding of desire and affection. I desired to be wanted, but not like that. Not by him. I felt dirty. Bad for what happened. Bad for the thoughts I began to have. Bad for keeping a secret. And so much more.

But no one else knew. I became a secret keeper.

— Sandi

Incongruent thoughts and feelings. I had never heard of that concept until Michelle identified it early on in our counseling sessions. To know the truth of a situation but to still carry from it a false, negative narrative.

• I know God loves me. I believe it. But I don't feel it.

- I know my husband and kids love me. But I feel unloved.
- I know it wasn't my fault, but I still feel dirty and ashamed.

Truth in one hand. A false, negative narrative in the other. Intellectually, you can discern the difference and identify truth, but emotionally, you land in a very negative place. That was the struggle.

I wish that identifying the struggle was the only step to healing. But it wasn't. The journey for me wasn't a clean, linear process—share a memory, gain insight, cry, and celebrate the win. That certainly happened. But the process of sharing your deepest pain and your darkest shame carries a lot of weight. It takes time to peel back the layers. To put words to the pain. To feel and process the emotions. To sort through truth and lies. It is emotionally, physically, and cognitively exhausting. Freedom is always costly.

Sharing my traumatic memory of sexual abuse with Michelle was beyond painful. I remember sitting in her office in silence because I struggled with putting words to what had happened. I would, for the first time, have to admit it. Face it. And I didn't know how to do that. The fear of putting syllables together was almost paralyzing. It felt like the pain wouldn't be real unless I said it out loud. But then it would get so real that I couldn't take it back or tuck it away again.

I knew I was being asked to let go of something. Part of me desperately wanted to. But it also felt like part of me was being ripped away. So, I held on tight.

At first, I simply sat. And sobbed. Obviously, I knew what had happened to me, and I knew it would be helpful to discuss it with Michelle. But I couldn't bring myself to do that. I had told no one. Ever. Not even my husband. I didn't want to say the word abuse. I didn't want to put words to what my stepfather had done. Or what I felt. The memory was clear. The feelings were intense. But the words wouldn't come. There was an immense amount of shame and fear of rejection.

I remember shaking my head as I wept. It wasn't intentional. It was a reaction, my body voicing its disdain. Everything in me wanted to stay inside: unseen, unheard, locked away.

I don't know what I feared most. Rejection? Judgment? Or feeling? Pain avoidance was in full-throttle mode. I didn't want to say it. I didn't want to feel it. I knew one would lead to the other. Finally, though, the emotional avalanche began.

"I was so stupid! I shouldn't have been sitting on his lap. What was I thinking? I should have screamed. Or told my mom. Or hit him. Why didn't I? How could he? How could I? It was all my fault. I'm so mad at myself!"

The words were loud as they came out of my mouth. The emotions on the inside felt even louder. I was mad. Embarrassed. Frustrated. Sad. Angry—mainly at myself. Harsh words poured out of me. Pent-up emotion. Decades of shame. I was mad at my stepfather for taking advantage of me. But the feelings had stayed inside and festered. Until somehow it all got misdirected, aimed at myself.

I was fair game because I had already believed I was unlovable.

My mind knew what had happened to me wasn't my fault, but my feelings weren't in sync. Shame won the debate. It had been speaking to me in a convincing way from the dark, and I'd believed it.

Now my painful secret had found the light of day. And in a word, I felt broken. Like I was literally snapped in two. As I shared the painful memory, I saw that picture in my mind—my stepfather snapping me in two, like a twig. It's what I saw. It's what I felt. Physically, emotionally, permanently broken. He had broken me from the inside out. Beyond repair.

Once the emotional avalanche subsided, I felt an odd mixture of exhaustion and finality. It didn't feel like the beginning of healing at all. I felt like I had reached the end of the road. I had said the words. I'd cried about it. And now what? It felt like a dead end.

I remember sitting in the counseling office thinking to myself, *There's nowhere to go from here. Broken is broken.* I honestly couldn't see a way out, no road to healing or even a path to better. Broken is what I knew. Better was beyond my ability to ponder.

I remember waiting for Michelle's response. Her reaction to me. I was prepared for an expression or a subtle shift in her body language that would tell me the truth I already knew, that I was bad.

It didn't happen. She didn't condemn or reject me. It looked like she had seen and heard stories like mine before. She was engaged, compassionate, and patient. What she didn't say spoke volumes to me.

As did her gentle response. "You're not broken, Sandi. You're wounded. And there's a difference."

We both sat in silence for a moment. I recall Michelle taking a deep breath. Slowly inhaling and exhaling. Was she breathing in everything I had just shared? Was she breathing to give some space to what was happening in the room? Or did she think I needed a cleansing breath and was hoping I would follow her lead? I did.

After another moment of trusted silence, I said, "One night after we finished dinner, I wanted to leave the table to go play. My stepdad said I couldn't leave until I said, 'May I be excused, sir?' I don't remember if he required my brother to say it or not. But I refused to say it. I was the only one sitting at the table for hours. I didn't throw a fit or cry. I simply sat. In silence. In rebellion. But . . . I finally gave in and said the words. It felt like he won. I'm not sure what I was fighting for, but it felt like I lost. Again."

As I sat across from Michelle, I remember feeling completely empty. Emotionally drained. I felt worthless. I was drowning anew in the emotion from these painful experiences. It felt heavy, like it was sitting on my shoulders and I was shrinking under the weight of it.

Michelle broke the silence. "I'm proud of that little girl. She was sticking up for herself and fighting back the only way she knew how. She was a fighter."

A fighter? I didn't see that one coming. Of all the things I expected her to say, of all the words I've used to describe myself, especially in light of what I'd just shared, that one didn't make my list. We were both looking at the same thing but drawing very different conclusions. I saw myself as stupid and broken. She saw a little fighter struggling to survive.

This profound realization was one I will never forget. She heard the "worst" about me and still believed I was worth fighting for. I was shocked. For the first time, I was able to get a glimpse of a six-year-old little girl who needed and deserved compassion and understanding. Not condemnation. I was beginning to see her through a lens of grace and truth. I was beginning to see truth and shame—and discern the difference.

Michelle ended with a pivotal question: "What would it look like for you to fight for yourself today?"

UNPACKING THE PROCESS
WITH DR. MICHELLE

Moving from Broken to Wounded

In that room that day, I saw the opportunity to offer life-giving words to Sandi. She had spent so long condemning her small self from decades ago that she had become utterly convinced of her perspective.

This is common, so common, in shame. If I can't blame someone else, who is left to blame?

We know foundationally that we're not supposed to blame or resent someone else or condemn them in our hearts. But we're fair game. Someone has to be responsible, and shame tells us that it should be ourselves. After all, if this is true, if we were responsible for the awful thing, then we can do everything in our power to prevent it from happening again, right? We can live carefully between the lines of shame.

That day, Sandi allowed me to gently flip the script. There is always, always a different perspective—one that can shine through as more truthful when not covered by shame and self-condemnation.

Memories and lingering messages are whispered into our souls. You may have some very painful ones circling in your mind and heart right now. You may have a sick feeling in your stomach. Or you may want to cry or run away. You are taking a courageous step right now. The first steps toward healing and fighting for freedom.

You might feel like you're too broken for healing. That there are too many pieces. Too many to sort, too many to put back together, too many to move forward from. If so, I invite you to consider *kintsugi*, the four-hundred-year-old Japanese art of putting broken pottery pieces back together. In *kintsugi*, the point isn't to cover the cracks and the broken places; the object is to highlight them, often with gold lacquer.

During my time as a hospice therapist, I worked with individuals, families, and kids who had been shattered by grief. Many felt utterly broken by the death of their loved ones, unable to put their lives back together. Some even felt shame, regret, and guilt in relationships with the ones they lost— leaving behind shards that felt like they couldn't be healed, no matter how much time had passed or how many tears were shed.

At a hospice grief camp, I had the privilege of witnessing families doing *kintsugi*. Each family member took a small hammer and gently smacked the side of a plain pottery jar until the pieces were left lying in a pile on the table. Then, working together, the family put the pieces back together with some lines of sticky glue. The pieces of the terracotta jar no longer fit seamlessly. Smaller pieces had turned to dust, leaving gaps. Some pieces were stuck in the wrong places. But the glue held it all together.

When the pottery jar was reassembled to some degree, each member of the family then painted a picture or word on it that represented their pain, their hope, their tribute. In the process of repairing this object that had looked broken—ready for the trash heap, in fact—they were creating something more unique and resilient. Something meaningful. Something beautiful.

You may feel utterly broken. I would suggest to you instead that you are wounded. You are still in the fight. Wounds can heal, even though there will be scars. We see beautiful evidence of this in Jesus's resurrection following the breaking of His body. John 20:19–31 tells us the story of how Jesus appeared to His disciples and showed them His healed scars, not once but twice. The scars not only showed Jesus's true identity but also reminded the disciples of all the pain they had been through in His last hours—the fear, the remorse, the grief they felt. His wounds were reminders of pain, but yet . . . they were overjoyed when they saw the Lord and His scars.

Does that mean we should be happy that we're wounded? By the nicks and bumps of childhood, the gouges of divorce, the deep wounds of betrayal. By the wrongs that have not been righted, harsh words that have a direct line to our hearts, and the memories that can't be erased.

I don't think so. That's not where the joy resides. The joy resides in the fact that Jesus shows us His wounds so we can see our own. So, we can know He gets us, our wounds, our hurt places. And know He loves us still. He can get through any amount of scar tissue.

I understand that, as a woman who loves God, you know deep down in your spirit that God didn't cause the thing that wounded you so deeply. A good hand doesn't do evil. But you may feel that He didn't see you that day. He didn't cause the painful event, but it doesn't feel like He was all that present either. He wasn't really paying attention to you.

While we are redefining ourselves—from, say, victim to fighter—we also need to redefine how we see God during our painful experiences. In those broken pieces where they feel unseen, unheard, just a little too small for God to notice them, I ask my clients to see the fullness of God. Can I ask you to remember as well? To see, again, His sovereignty and omniscience, but also His omnipresence and compassion for you. Of knowing that Jesus didn't just suffer and ascend to heaven all healed and good, He still bears the scars because He knows and feels the scars. He kept them so He would never forget you and your wounded places. He kept them out of compassion for you.

Working through the pain means that it's no longer hidden. It opens the possibility of compassion—for yourself and from God and others. Compassion means looking at your pain from a different perspective, one that is more truthful and present. It means that the kindness of your heart—the same heart you would offer to a friend, right?—is ready to challenge those old messages gently.

Looking at the scars may help you realize there's more to the story.

There's bravery.

There's resiliency.

There's compassion.

There could be joy.

REFLECTION

There is a redemptive thought in moving from a view of being utterly broken to being wounded. Wounds, thankfully, have great power to heal. Can you allow some space for a different definition of who you are?

When you think about a wounded person, what image comes to mind? When you think about a brave person, what image comes to mind? Can a wounded person and a brave person be one and the same?

_____

_____

Take a moment to write a few words describing yourself in your painful story. Now, consider a compassionate friend's perspective. What words would they use?

_____

_____

What characteristics did you miss feeling or knowing about God during your painful experiences? Are you acknowledging the fullness of His character, including His compassion for you? How can you know Him for all of His characteristics? How can you trust Jesus with your scar tissue today?

_____

_____

SCRIPTURE

"Those who sow with tears
will reap with songs of joy."

— Psalm 126:5

"'Though the mountains be shaken and the hills be
removed, yet my unfailing love for you will not be
shaken nor my covenant of peace be removed,'
says the LORD, who has compassion on you."

— Isaiah 54:10

"Record my misery; list my tears on your scroll—
are they not in your record?
Then my enemies will turn back
when I call for help. By this I
will know that God is for me."

— Psalm 56:8–9

PRAYER

God, this feels like too big of a box to open. I'm getting to the source, and I'm scared. I feel too broken and not too brave. But I am relying on Your strength, Your courage, and Your love to see me through. I see we both have scars, and those scars came through the most difficult of places. My trust is in Your healing. Help me see myself as You see me—as someone who is capable of bravery when I want to run in the other direction and someone who is resilient when I don't think I can do this anymore. Grant me compassion where there may be resentment and give me joy that only comes from You. Thank You, Jesus, for Your scars and for Your healing.

HEALING MAP

3

Identify the Impact of Your Pain

4

Look at Your Pain with Compassion and Truth

5

Make Choices About Your Memories

Chapter 5

MEMORY BAG

Email to Michelle:

Good morning. Sorry to bother you. I'm struggling a bit. After our meeting yesterday, I was emotionally spent, so I took a nap. I just felt sick to my stomach and "off." I spent time in my Bible, but it was like the words were jumbled and disconnected. Gobbledygook—that's what my brain feels like and even what some of my sentences sound like. Pretty strange.

Concentration has been a real challenge. Haven't felt this before. Had a rough/interrupted night of sleep. Is this normal?

Michelle's response:

Dear Sandi,

I am so glad you reached out. I know it is probably distressing to feel the physical symptoms as well as the mind jumble, but please know this is a normal physiological outcome of talking through what you shared in the session.

I suspect that the stress hormone cortisol was released.

When that happens, adrenaline (that's the fight-or-flight hormone) kicks up. And once that's done, it can leave you feeling nauseous and tired. It's our bodies functioning as they were built by God to evade a threat, and your memory was the "threat" that kicked off the stress. Trauma is also retained in the body, and I suspect you might have been identifying with what you felt at the time that it occurred.

There are several things that can help. First, breathe deeply. Second, if you can, move your body! One of the best ways to alleviate this feeling is through a walk, some stretching, etc.

Please know this doesn't mean you should not have shared what you did. It is simply your body's natural release of what has been held in for so long, and most likely it will continue to improve throughout the day. Know that I'm praying this is the case.

Like a thousand-piece puzzle scattered across the table. With hundreds of missing pieces. That is how I felt throughout the first several months of counseling. I was putting my life on the table, full disclosure, but it wasn't all fitting together like I thought it would or should. There were aha moments of clarity when pieces came together. Those made sense. They brought peace. I was hopeful. And yet there was an overarching impression that there was more "undone" than "done" in my life.

Unresolved pain was evident. The pieces had been there for years, but they'd been carefully tucked away, kept in the box—ignored, really. But at least they'd been contained. Now they lay exposed. In the open. I had to look at them, feel them, and try to make sense of them.

Wayne Muller, a therapist and author of Legacy of the Heart, noted, "As long as we hold onto how this or that person hurt or dishonored us, we are trapped in a dance of suffering with that person forever." For me, it felt as though I was trapped in a highly emotional dance with myself and others. And then there were days like the one I described in the email to Michelle that hit me out of nowhere. My mind, heart, and body felt completely out of sync as I uncovered and examined my past pain. It was unsettling.

Michelle explained there was purpose in processing through the memories and painful experiences. One of those purposes was to realize we have a choice in how we deal with the pain today. We can learn from it. We can release it. We can carry some of it with us. We have a say in all of those choices. That was needed encouragement for the unfamiliar road ahead.

Still, although the counseling work felt meticulous and intentional, it was not always linear and clean. I guess pain rarely is. I'm sure that as a counselor, Michelle understood the process to processing. I won't pretend to know the nuances of how it all works, but I will try to explain what it felt like from my side of the couch: like a rollercoaster ride through a tornado. Highs, lows, turns, screams, anticipation, fear . . . But I didn't have my hands in the air. I was holding on for dear life.

Before Michelle and I began processing the memories, I

shared with her that I have a lot of blank spaces in my mind. I was thirteen years old when my mom and stepdad divorced. I have very few memories from age six to thirteen. I don't remember what my room looked like, my childhood friends, my first days of school, or holidays. When I try to remember our family during that time, I just picture the inside of our house as being dark and stuffy. Joyless. Scary.

I was struggling with the fact that I had so few memories. I was concerned that if the truth sets you free, and I couldn't remember the truth, would I ever find freedom?

Michelle suggested I pray and ask God to bring to mind any memories that were necessary and helpful for healing. That's what I did. For days. Weeks. And nothing new came to mind. At first, I was frustrated and disappointed. I thought the only way to complete the puzzle of my life and to heal was to put all of the pieces together methodically. Clearly, there were missing pieces and memories.

During that time, God lovingly reminded me that facts and memories aren't the keys to freedom. He is the way, the truth, and the life. Freedom comes from Him and through Him (see John 14:6). I believe it was a trust-fall moment for me. Was I seeking answers, or was I trusting Him as the source of my freedom? He reminded me of His trustworthy character: "The LORD is my rock, my fortress and my deliverer; my God is my rock, in whom I take refuge" (Psalm 18:2).

The word protection stood out and resonated with me. Was my lack of memory recall a self-protective subconscious act? I don't know. And I don't understand why God didn't restore the memories. But I do know He is my protector. I trust that if additional memories are needed to more fully heal, then He will give them to me. And I trust that if He is protecting my mind and heart in a different way, then I am thankful. Either way, He is faithful.

With that reassurance in mind, I began walking down the road of processing the memories with Michelle. She suggested we take some deep breaths. She explained that it would calm any physical responses that might occur as part of bringing up a memory. Even thinking about a past trauma can trigger a threat response like fight, flee, or freeze mode. So, Michelle had me take deep breaths and asked me to check in with any physical responses that came up as we processed.

At that point we were ready to work through visualizing my memories and identifying the emotions attached to them. Scary, yes! But the idea was to look at the experiences honestly and truthfully, with all of the feelings and visuals they contained, and release them so they were no longer "stuck" in place and affecting me negatively. A way of letting the "loud" out.

The exercise was to imagine I was walking over a bridge while carrying a large bag. The bag represented a past traumatic memory I had been carrying around (like when my dad left or when I was later abused). The bridge represented a path that moved me away from the painful experience and toward a different future.

Once in the middle of the bridge, Michelle had me picture opening the bag. She asked me to see what emotions were present with my memory, giving me the chance to describe those feelings: things like sadness . . . anger . . . anticipation.

Then Michelle began to ask questions about the memory, encouraging me to drill down to the connections between it and the emotions I carried in my bag. Before the exercise ended, there were two important questions to consider:

- What do you want to release and leave behind?
- What are you choosing to take with you as you move forward in healing?

This was a new concept for me—choices—and as we worked through the memory and emotions, I came to understand that I have a say in the healing process. I may not have had a say in what was originally put into my bag (the specific trauma), but I do get to decide what to do with it now, what I want to leave behind, and what I want to take with me as I move forward.

Here is what I chose to leave behind. These things were not going back into my bag:

X *Unfair untruths.* The beliefs that I am unwanted and unlovable.

X *Negative self-assessment.* Any shameful lie that contradicts the truth and leads to condemnation.

X *Shame about what happened.* Something bad happened to me, but that does not mean I am bad.

X *Unforgiveness.* Bitterness toward anyone in my past. Toward myself.

X *A refusal to let go.* I held onto the pain so tightly. Or maybe it had a hold of me. Either way, I didn't realize how much energy it took from me.

Who would want to carry those things around? Not me. Not anymore. I pictured myself naming and throwing each uninvited item off the bridge. It was a visual release of emotions and beliefs that had been weighing me down for far too long. I saw each one descending farther and farther away from me until it splashed into the water below and sank beyond my ability to see it. The memory in my bag was still there, but the connected emotions were gone, no longer mine to carry. I had let go of them all.

The next step was to identify what, if anything, I wanted to put into my bag and carry with me as I left. Was there any gained insight that would be helpful and necessary as I move forward? Here is what I pictured putting into the bag:

- ✔ *Compassion.* I have asked God to give me compassion and concern for those who have hurt me. I don't want to be hard-hearted toward them. Or myself.

- ✔ *Understanding.* I will look at my life through the lens of truth. I was hurt. My feelings are normal.

- ✔ *Knowledge that I am loved.* My dad wasn't capable of loving me the way I needed him to. I wish he had. But just because he didn't love me well doesn't mean I am unlovable.

- ✔ *Self-control.* I am not tethered to anyone who did me harm. Any sort of hold or control they may have had over me is over. They, or their actions, will not define me.

✔ *Grace*. I will show grace to myself. I am not broken. I was wounded. But I am healing.

✔ *Hope*. I carry faith in God's goodness. For me. For my future. For eternity.

I know this process was merely a mental exercise, but I could almost immediately feel the difference in the weight I carried. I paused to thank God. Was I casting my emotions, my cares, and my burdens into the water or into His hands? It didn't really matter. Either way, I was no longer carrying them.

As odd as it may sound, the walk back over and off the bridge was also meaningful. To me, it represented movement, a clear delineation of "there" and "here" in my mind and heart and the hard-fought journey in between. Yes, pain, shame, and regret are "there," but I'm no longer there. I'm "here" now, walking with truth, insight, and understanding.

I took that journey across the bridge multiple times under Michelle's watchful care. Each bridge encounter with each traumatic memory was different, yet emotional and insightful. The items tossed and the ones carried with me varied. But the one constant was God's presence. He showed up every time. In the scene of the memory. On the edge of the bridge. Encouraging me in the journey. He was present. And He wanted my heart to know: He was carrying me and my bag.

One time I even saw my husband, Mike, on the bridge. It was unexpected and powerful for him to meet me "there." And walk with me. Another gift my heart needed to know.

To be perfectly honest, I started each processing session with a fair amount of skepticism. Visualizing . . .

imagining . . . bridges and bags. It all sounded a bit . . . unfamiliar. Perhaps that's where you are as you read this now. If so, I encourage you to trust the process. I didn't understand how talking about a memory that had brought me pain for decades would change anything. But it did, bit by bit. It was another important step in the healing process.

The pain feels diluted now, after the bridge exercise. The memory is still in my bag. I remember clearly the trauma that we discussed. But the pain isn't the only thing in my bag. There is also an understanding that I am loved. There is grace, compassion, and hope. My bag is full—with the right emotions. The load feels lighter.

UNPACKING THE PROCESS
WITH DR. MICHELLE

Looking Inside the Bag

Here's the thing: no one welcomes pain into her life. No one throws her arms open wide to revisit the pain of childhood (or yesterday). As we've previously discussed, we are built to avoid pain. Even though we can sense we are carrying a big, heavy bag full of stuff, we may hesitate to look inside, much less unpack it.

Maybe like Sandi, you've realized that you don't need to or simply don't want to carry your burden anymore. The burden might feel familiar in your arms because you've been carrying it so long. You might even believe you deserve the pain it brings; it's proof behind those old messages you've been listening to. But when you picked up this book, you were at the point that you needed to hear something different. See something different about yourself. Know something different, down into your heart and up into your mind.

It might be more than you bargained for, like it was for Sandi when she first walked into the counseling room. She couldn't have seen this coming. Really, there was no way to warn her about how tough this process would be. She might have run away, and who would have blamed her? The best she and I could do was to create a place of safety. Safety in the counseling room to feel all the feels. Safety in her relationship with God, knowing He felt every bit of sorrow, every bit of grief, every bit of anger that she was feeling.

When we can create some of that safety, within the privacy of the pages of this book or with a trusted person, we can begin to process and release some of the traumatic experiences and the mental/emotional jumble that naturally follows. When we are stressed or have experienced trauma, there are all sorts of normal reactions: physical, emotional, and cognitive.

Physical

As Sandi mentioned, when we processed her memories in a different way, her body went on high alert—similar to what her body originally experienced during her childhood. Our bodies are memory keepers! Bessel van der Kolk writes in *The Body Keeps the Score*:

Trauma victims cannot recover until they become familiar with and befriend the sensations in their bodies. Being frightened means that you live in a body that is always on guard . . . In order to change, people need to become aware of their sensations and the way that their bodies interact with the world around them. Physical self-awareness is the first step in releasing the tyranny of the past.

There are several ways to bring physical self-awareness and to care for yourself in this process:

- Breathe deeply. When we are in an alerted state, we breathe from the top of our chests. This is survival breathing! When you breathe deeply from your stomach all the way up through your lungs, you are telling the body that the threat isn't real. You can even "breathe" Jesus, visualizing Him as the breath in your lungs and your calming presence.

- Use a bilateral movement. Bilateral movements are any repeated movement done on both sides of the body, which can instantly help you relax. Bilateral movements include moving your eyes back and forth (like we do in REM sleep), tapping your right leg with your right hand and vice versa, or alternating between squeezing a stress ball in each hand.

- Move your body. Take a walk in the sunshine and feel the air on your skin. Stretch from your chair, feeling the pops and the loosening of tense muscles.

Check in with yourself before and after to see the differences in tension held in your body.

- Use grounding techniques. One of my clients' favorites is the five senses:

1. Notice five things you can see. Pause and really see them.

2. Notice four things you can feel. Feel the texture. Is it soft? Hard? Rough? Smooth?

3. Notice three things you can hear. Listen to the birds, traffic, or voices for a moment.

4. Notice two things you can smell. Are they pleasant smells? Unpleasant?

5. Notice one thing you can taste. Even if it's just your saliva! If you need to grab some gum or food to taste, that's fine. Pause and enjoy the flavor.

Emotional

The emotional piece is just as important in processing memories. In counseling, I know we are making progress in resolving pain when emotions are felt and expressed. Too often we are taught very early on that certain—or all—emotions are bad. Told to keep them locked up. *Keep smiling, girls. Keep the tears in until you can get to your closet.*

When the emotion box is opened, that becomes the first beautiful step toward looking at the pain honestly. It's no longer just a story but part of *your* story, one that can be told with all of the elements, including sadness, grief, loneliness, doubt, indignation, fear. There is truthfulness in these raw emotions. Yes, we're capable of great joy, happiness, contentment, and peace—all those emotions we want—but part of the deal is that we're also capable of great distress. We don't get one without the other.

At times, our emotional reactions can sit at the root of why we believed lies for so long.

- Someone told you that you made a bad decision, so you feel stupid.
- Someone left you, so you feel like a reject.
- Someone told you that you failed, so you feel worthless.
- Someone told you that you were bad, so you feel shame.

I'm the first one, as a counselor, to say that emotions are the spice of life. We can relate better to God if we feel some of the same emotions He does. After all, He has been livid, tearful, irritated, joyful, satisfied—if anyone has felt the feels, it's God. And as we learned earlier, God also gave emotions as useful indicators. If we feel good, whatever we're doing at the time should probably continue. If something feels painful or difficult, then it needs to change. If we're fearful, for example, we instinctively get ready to fight, flee, or freeze. (How useful when a bear comes into our campground looking for a snack!)

While we feel this range of emotions for great purpose, we should not allow them to create and establish our identity.

As mothers everywhere have said, just because you feel like it, doesn't mean it's true! Emotions and feelings can easily move into utter convictions. This is particularly true when we hear an early message or a lie about ourselves. We may feel it's valid in the moment—even if it isn't. And over time, and usually in a very sneaky manner, it becomes an unhealthy conviction. For example, instead of believing the promise of 2 Corinthians 5:17 that "the old has gone, the new is here," we may decide that a bad past equals a bad future.

We can choose to uncover those nasty, harmful, utterly untrue convictions and to challenge them, to replace them with the truth about who we are. As one of my clients so insightfully said, "I'm not letting a feeling be the period at the end of the sentence."

Not stupid.

Not rejected.

Not worthless.

Not shameful.

Cognitive

Once we have drawn out the memories, we can process them and make choices about how we think of them. As van der Kolk notes, "As long as you keep secrets and suppress information, you are fundamentally at war with yourself . . . The critical issue is allowing yourself to know what you know. That takes an enormous amount of courage." It's courageous to stand in the middle of a bridge, process the memories, and decide what goes and what stays. It means you are no longer helpless. No longer completely out of control. You can leave behind lies, emotions, and thoughts that are not welcome in your mind and heart. Now you are on the healing path as you explore these questions, holding your own experiences with compassion and curiosity, rather than condemnation.

Here are a few questions to contemplate as you consider your process of moving a memory forward:

- What do you want to keep with you as you move forward in a healthy way?
- What do you feel was hard earned, learned, or valuable?
- What is the good you can take with you?
- What do you choose to leave behind?

We may have believed the lie that we can't control our feelings of shame, guilt, anger, or fear, and that we have to live under the storm cloud of our painful experiences forever. The truth is we are called to know in our hearts and minds that we're no longer condemned to living at the whim of our feelings. The Message translates this reminder so wonderfully:

> *With the arrival of Jesus, the Messiah, that fateful dilemma is resolved. Those who enter into Christ's being-here-for-us no longer have to live under a continuous, low-lying black cloud. A new power is in operation. The Spirit of life in Christ, like a strong wind, has magnificently cleared the air, freeing you from a fated lifetime of brutal tyranny at the hands of sin and death.*
> *— Romans 8:1*

Oftentimes, we need to process these types of memories with a trained guide to help. If you are experiencing distressing symptoms that are interfering with your life and functioning, please connect with a counselor. There are many evidence-based therapeutic approaches to processing trauma, including Eye Movement Desensitization and Reprocessing (EMDR), Accelerated Resolution Therapy (ART), and Somatic Experiencing, among others. In the back of the book, you will find resources that will help you connect with a therapist. I hope you will take that step.

REFLECTION

This chapter begins the hard battle of negative convictions versus truth and shows us how we can process through our pain to see what lies beyond. The steps to process the painful memories include: (1) identifying what's contained in our bodies, (2) feeling the emotions and identifying truths and untruths, and (3) working through the memories themselves and seeing what we want to leave behind and what we want to take with us. As we journeyed together to uncover the myriad messages, lies, and emotions that were connected to Sandi's earliest experiences, she recorded her realizations. Perhaps you had realizations of truth, as well, that you would like to record below. We invite you to prayerfully add your own. What have you been carrying for far too long, and what would you like to carry forward?

When you sit with your body for a moment, what physical sensations come up? Where do you feel tension, anxiety, etc.? What can you do to calm the physical sensation?

_____

_____

What are some of the lies about yourself that you have carried with you, in your bag, all this time? (As a reminder, Sandi's were feeling abandoned and rejected, negative self-assessment, shame about what happened, and confusion and difficulty releasing the pain.)

_____

_____

What can you choose to leave behind today as you process through past hurts? What are you throwing over the side of the bridge?

_____

_____

What helpful truths are you taking with you? (As a reminder, Sandi's were compassion, understanding, knowledge that she is loved, control of self, and grace.)

_____

_____

SCRIPTURE

"Come to me, all you who are weary and burdened, and I will give you rest. Take my yoke upon you and learn from me, for I am gentle and humble in heart, and you will find rest for your souls. For my yoke is easy and my burden is light."

— MATTHEW 11:28–30

"He holds success in store for the upright, he is a shield to those whose walk is blameless, for he guards the course of the just and protects the way of his faithful ones."

— PROVERBS 2:7–8

"When I said, 'My foot is slipping,' your unfailing love, LORD, supported me. When anxiety was great within me, your consolation brought me joy."

— Psalm 94:18–19

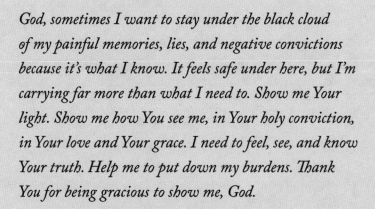

PRAYER

God, sometimes I want to stay under the black cloud of my painful memories, lies, and negative convictions because it's what I know. It feels safe under here, but I'm carrying far more than what I need to. Show me Your light. Show me how You see me, in Your holy conviction, in Your love and Your grace. I need to feel, see, and know Your truth. Help me to put down my burdens. Thank You for being gracious to show me, God.

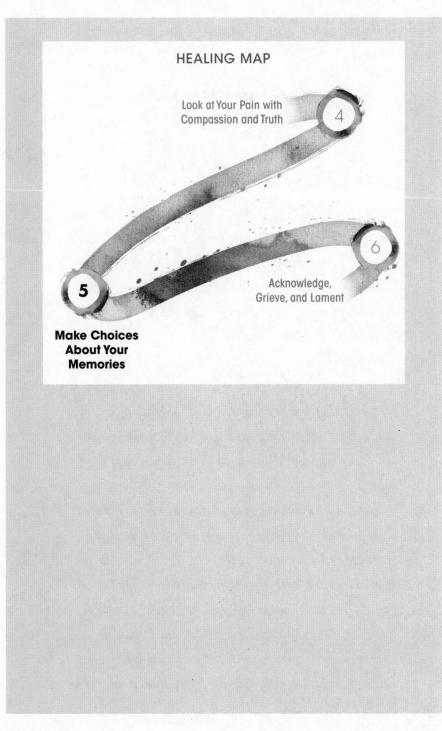

Chapter 6

LOST AND FOUND

Yesterday I drove by the house where we lived with my stepdad. I don't know why. Conflicting thoughts were bouncing around in my mind. My heart started racing. What am I doing here? Part of me hoped he would be outside so I could see him. The other part prayed he wasn't. That prayer was answered.

The house looked the same. Like nothing had changed. I immediately felt like I was ten years old again. Thinking of the days, nights, and years spent in that house made me sad. Realizing I'm still drawn to it today made me cry.

Last night I looked at old pictures of my dad. They were given to me when he passed away. Pictures from before I knew him. A few pictures of us together. Reminders that even though he was part of my life for twenty-six years, he never knew me. I wished he had. There were so many unmet expectations. Unfulfilled longings. Missed opportunities. It was sad when he died. But last night, the pain was different. I felt a deep ache in my heart.

Tonight, I'm reflecting on everything that has been lost. I'm not only sad for my six-year-old self. I'm drowning in the realization that my life today is tethered to the past in a zillion different painful ways.

I asked Michelle why I'm feeling this way. Why am I so sad about things that happened so long ago? Will I ever get past it all? It feels like it's overshadowing the tastes of freedom that I'm discovering. It feels like I'm carrying both sadness and freedom together. How is that possible? I'm concerned I'm going to get stuck in the sad.

Michelle said, "Sandi, sad is when you recognize the hurt. Grief is when you feel the loss. You are grieving what was lost."

– Sandi

"Grief is normal. Grief is good," Michelle said. She assured me that the deep, persistent emotions I was feeling were a necessary part of the healing process. The journey, as Michelle will explain later in this chapter, has two important steps: (1) acknowledging past hurts and (2) grieving and lamenting.

I had acknowledged my past hurts, out loud. Now I was walking through the grief stage, and it was new territory for me. Although this emotional release felt a bit overwhelming, Michelle said that in time I would eventually come through to the other side of grief. She also said that experiencing sorrow and sadness is good. It means the heart is alive—no longer numb. It means healthy feelings are returning, including empathy. She said having compassion for someone is good and appropriate, even if that someone is yourself.

It was helpful to view this season as necessary and productive to the overall goal, otherwise it would have just been torturous and painful. Michelle explained that when you allow yourself to feel the pain of your losses, there is an honest alignment. Your feelings are appropriate and begin to connect with the truth. For years I had tried to ignore past hurts and to stuff my emotions, but that wasn't a useful or appropriate response to pain. Wounds equal sadness. That is how congruency is fostered. I needed to give myself permission to grieve my hurts.

So, I did. It wasn't easy. But I began to see this experience as valuable sadness. It was costing me something, but that is often true when obtaining something valuable.

I remember when Michelle first asked if I was ready to consider, "What was lost?" That felt quite different than discussing a past experience. At first, I couldn't articulate why. But I think it was because a memory was something my mind saw clearly contained in the past. There was a sense of detachment. But a loss? There was no denying I was still very much attached to it.

I sat down with my journal and asked God for help. I asked Him to reveal the areas of my life that were defined by loss. The areas still tethered to past hurts and wounds. I wasn't looking for more pain. But I did want a full measure of understanding, which hopefully would lead to a full measure of freedom. I wanted to touch the bottom of the pool so I could come up for air.

Here is what I wrote:

What Was Lost?

- *A carefree childhood*
- *A healthy self-image and self-confidence*
- *A sense of being okay*
- *An ability to trust appropriately*
- *A feeling of security in relationships. I learned from my dad and stepdad that love had to be earned and transactional. That meant I never felt safe.*
- *Appropriate affection/physical touch from dad/stepdad: hugs, holding my hand, hearing "I love you" and "I'm proud of you"*
- *Trust and understanding of intimacy, both physically and relationally*
- *Physical and emotional innocence. Abuse opened a door that should have remained closed, especially to a little girl. Love, intimacy, touch, pleasure—all distorted.*
- *Memories. Years of good and normal things. Special occasions. Joyful times with friends or extended family.*
- *An apology. I never heard "I'm sorry" from those who hurt me.*
- *A desire for vulnerability*
- *Friendships. I was afraid to let anyone get too close.*
- *Sleep. I still have dreams with a recurring theme.*

The exercise was difficult and emotional. It is one thing to know your past. Quite another to see how the dominoes have fallen and impacted every area of your life today. I was starting to understand just how deep the water was. That was both troubling and necessary.

And yet, the exercise also allowed me to experience something else. Before writing everything down, the loss had seemed overwhelming and endless, like I was drowning in sadness. I was feeling hopeless. But as odd as it sounds, once on paper, I could see the bottom. There was a sense of containment—a beginning and an end—that brought some peace. There was an honest alignment with my thoughts and emotions. They were in sync.

The result was appropriate grief for all that was lost and a sense of relief in understanding what was happening.

One day, during this season of grief, my phone rang. It was a family member sharing that my uncle, my dad's brother, was in the hospital. Even though he lived a couple of hours away, he had been admitted to a hospital near my work. We hadn't seen each other in a long time, but I was eager to visit him. I remembered him as being funny, rough on the outside, but more tenderhearted than he wanted to admit.

I had forgotten how much his face and hands looked like my dad's.

"Why do I cry every time I see you?" I said as I walked into his hospital room. We both laughed through a tear or two.

Over the following days, we enjoyed this unexpected opportunity to reconnect. The daily visits to the hospital were intended to lift his spirits, but they were an unexpected gift to my soul. They were full of conversation, laughter, and a few more tears. I learned about his love for cookies, his wife, family, and God. Not necessarily in that order.

Each visit ended with, "I love you." And I believed him.

During one of our chats, I sat on the side of the bed. We were delving into some matters of the heart, and he reached out and took my hand. Immediately, I started to cry. There was something so powerful about seeing those hands holding mine. In an instant, I was reconnecting with my younger self and grieving that my father's hands had never held mine the way my uncle's did now.

My uncle must have sensed some of what I was feeling. He said, "Sandi, I'm sorry about your daddy. I want you to know that I always wished I could have been your dad."

My uncle will never know the fullness of what he gave me that day. I got to see a father's heart. I felt a father's love—emotionally and physically. I was known. And wanted.

God was the only one who knew what my heart needed in that season. During that time of contemplating loss, He was so kind to tend to my heart. The timing . . . the words . . . the encouragement . . . all orchestrated by God. My uncle was simply the hands of Jesus that day to a heart that was grieving.

That is how I know you can carry both grief and hope. Fully. One doesn't need to cancel out the other. Both are helpful in the healing journey, and the God of all hope and comfort comes closest when our hearts are breaking.

UNPACKING THE PROCESS
WITH DR. MICHELLE

Acknowledging, Grieving, and Lamenting the Losses

It is an understandable, seemingly noble, strategy: avoid past pain and wounds, and try to keep the past in the past. Move on, be brave, be better. Pull yourself up by the bootstraps. Who wants the alternative? Feel all the feels, get stuck in the sadness, and live in the past.

Here's the danger to stuffing, avoiding, dodging past pain: it still squishes out, even daily and over a lifetime. It affects relationships. It can make us snarky and cynical, distrustful, and unloving. We need to see and acknowledge, grieve, and actively lament the small and great losses behind the painful experience to truly move in freedom and peace.

One day I was rushing around trying to leave for church. I ran into the laundry room, found a clean dress, threw it over my head, and whirled toward stepping over the baby gate. But my graceful pirouette turned into a flailing of arms and legs as the hem of my dress caught on the gate. Then down I went to the hardwood floor into a less-than-elegant face-plant.

After assessing for a moment, I realized I had broken my elbow. Broken. My. Elbow.

I was tempted to lie there on the floor and wait. Ignore the pain. Save the expense of going to the doctor. Not interrupt the preparations I knew were going on at church. Bottom line, I didn't want to bother anybody, even as I lay there in excruciating pain.

But as the dog came to lick my face in sympathy—but didn't understand my Lassie-go-get-my-phone instructions—I realized I'd have to get some help. I needed to acknowledge I wasn't on my way to church but rather on the way to a doctor. The pain radiating up my arm was proof that something was badly wrong and needed attention. I had to understand what was going on so I had the potential of fixing it now rather than allowing it to become an even more painful problem down the road.

I got up, cradled my arm, and faced the X-ray and the discomfort of the cast whose purpose was solely to help me heal. None of this was easy!

Nowadays, discomfort in my arm still arises here and there. My elbow hurts slightly on a rainy day. (I've turned into a forty-something-year-old complaining about her joints when it's humid!) It signals to me that even now I need to pay attention to that pain. It's telling me something: that once I was wounded. I chose to seek healing, though, and the healing journey was worth it.

Just like physical pain, it isn't good to ignore emotional pain. Although they may not be visible, there are still wounds. Leaving them to fester unhealed isn't fair, and it isn't helpful in the healing journey.

Choosing to acknowledge and process your hurts and losses is a good thing, for a few reasons:

- *It is truthful.* Truth and freedom go hand in hand. As Jesus wisely declared, "The truth will set you free" (John 8:32). The enemy of your soul loves the dark, the lies, and the secrets. God celebrates and honors the truth.

- *It is compassionate.* Remember the story of the Good Samaritan? A traveler was attacked, robbed, and beaten. Some ignored the wounded one. But a Samaritan had compassion, bandaged the traveler's wounds, and paid for his care. Jesus said, "Go and do likewise" (Luke 10:37). You are your own Samaritan.

- *It is how your thoughts and emotions come into alignment.* Unresolved pain and the underlying losses may have resulted in perceptions and feelings that are negative and condemning. Honest, compassionate processing helps you discern the difference between truthful feelings and shameful thoughts. Congruent thoughts and emotions are rooted in the truth.

There is something almost holy about acknowledging the truth, especially when we don't want to, whatever the reason is. For instance, after Adam and Eve sinned in the Garden of Eden (see Genesis 3), they hid from God in shame. God pursued them with a question, "Where are you?" Of course, God already knew the answer. So why did He ask? Because He was inviting them to acknowledge the truth. Because we can only walk in truth once we acknowledge what has happened and where we are.

Our instinct may be to hide, to tuck away the pain and grief, to dismiss it, or to refuse to admit it. After all, who wants to acknowledge past hurts or wounds? God already sees our wounds, and He knows that the path forward begins with a loving question: "Where are you?" It's good for our souls to acknowledge and speak the truth. It's a surrendering which, I believe, God honors.

Still, for as natural and as human a process it is, I find that most of my clients are wary of acknowledging the past because it means they must experience the weight of grief. In all honesty, I don't blame them one bit. Grief hurts. More accurately, grief aches—a bone-wearying, heartbreaking kind of ache.

Why would someone in their right mind go through that?

Because without it, we risk staying in the place of our pain.

Let's look at an analogy for the process of grieving. Think of the loss as a countertop with sharp edges. It's right in the middle of your kitchen, where you do all of your food prepping and cooking. You try to avoid bumping into that countertop, but it's impossible. You keep running into it, bruising yourself over and over again. It may take you off guard. You were thinking about something else, and yet, there it was—sharp edges causing black-and-blue bruises.

Eventually, you recognize that the countertop is a part of your life and that it's quite functional. At that point you have two choices: (1) you can continue to try to give the counter a wide berth to keep from hurting yourself, but also lose out on its usefulness or (2) you can sand down the sharp edges so you no longer have to avoid it and are no longer in danger of the bumps and bruises.

Yes, it might be easier just to avoid it, but good, meaningful grief work means that you sand down the edges on that countertop so they're not quite so sharp. The countertop is still there, and that's okay. It's fine to still have that big thing present in your life. The grief work takes the edge off of it and allows you to find some peace around the kitchen. You can walk straight through the space without fear.

Grieving is also an immense act of love. We grieve because we have loved something or someone that is now gone. If we didn't care, we wouldn't mourn. As such, grieving love lost is an amazingly powerful tool; if you're grieving, that means what was lost is worthy of love, not shame. It means you're giving voice to your losses. It may be a loss of innocence, the loss of an ideal, or the loss of a part of yourself. Whatever the reason, grieving means you give space to recognize the impact that loss has on your life today. You, and anyone you ask to be present with you, can simply stand as witnesses. No judgment, just love.

So, what do we do with all of this grief? It has to go somewhere, right? One of the routes of grief expression and work that God has given us is the practice of lament. Lamenting is simply an emotional, honest, and vulnerable expression of your sorrow for what was lost.

Lament leads us deeper into the inmost heart of God, who grieves before, with, and even long after us. If you've been struggling with talking to God about your pain, you're not alone. God gives us some clues in the Bible about how difficult it is to grieve losses that don't make sense. We see many instances of lament in the Bible, such as Judah's pain-filled wailing and absolute desolation that took place following the fall of Jerusalem. This story makes up an entire book, Lamentations, dedicated to the process of mourning before the Lord. If an entire book of the Bible is dedicated to helping us know what to do when the bad stuff happens, that means it's important to God, right?

In Lamentations, the people sorrowfully cry out in response to the very real, tangible destruction of an entire city. Your losses may not feel so tangible but more under the surface. However, we can learn and apply a very similar process to help recognize, express, and move through our grief and losses from our past pain. Lament helps crack the door open to a healthy grieving progression. Lament can help give structure, purpose, and reassurance that you are moving through your grieving process.

All that said, how do we grieve those intangible losses? Although this isn't an exact road map of how to lament, the outline below provides a few helpful steps. Two key thoughts before you start: First, your lament process is going to be as unique as your losses. Second, you may move back and forth between these steps, revisiting each as needed. Grief and lament are not linear processes (unfortunately!), but you will honor yourself and your losses as you work through these steps in whatever fashion you need to.

- Recognize your suffering and losses.
  Reading Lamentations is a great place to start.
- Cry out to God. "Do You hear me, God? Can You handle what I have? Do You see my loss?"
- Complain and petition God. Voice to Him your resistance to your losses; He knows them well and can handle your feelings of struggle. But also, call out in the hope that things will change.
- Profess trust in God. Begin with a heart of expectation. Express, and in return, experience confidence that God is receiving your words.
- Receive words of reassurance. God sees you, and He desires to comfort you in your grief. Ask for the only kind of reassurance He can give you: complete and peaceful.
- Vow to praise God in the storm. Feel gratitude that God receives your losses, your pain, and your grief. He bends down to listen as you lament (see Psalm 116:2).

Unresolved pain doesn't usually lay dormant in your life. It can seep into the foundation of your soul. It is painful to acknowledge. The loss is real and is worth grieving and lamenting over, and it may have consequences that wreak havoc in a lot of areas in your life. The journey forward may take longer than you like. It may be costly. But (take a deep breath here), "He who began a good work in you will carry it on to completion" (Philippians 1:6).

God is doing a good work in your life. You can trust His handiwork, His timing, and His leading. He starts with where you are. He comes close to your broken heart. And He begins a transformation process in your life that only He can complete. He turns mourning into dancing. Sadness into joy. Broken into mended.

He could do it all in an instant. But if He did, we might miss the richness of His working, His presence, His comfort, and His healing.

REFLECTION

Identifying your "pain point" (or points) is the first step in beginning the healing process. This in itself is a process to identify where it hurts and—even more deeply—why it hurts. Then we can begin to understand our losses and how we have reacted to the absences in our lives. Take a moment to reflect on your process so far, and how you might continue to grieve and lament in a purposeful, God-honoring way.

Where are you in your processing: acknowledging the past hurts, grieving and lamenting, or correlating the past pain to your life today? How might you move forward to the next step?

_____

_____

What has prevented you from acknowledging your pain and losses?

_____

_____

God despises losses and death even more than we do. He says we will be comforted and blessed in our mourning (see Matthew 5:4). How can you receive comfort today?

_____

_____

Where do you think your pain shows in your life today? You can use Sandi's list as a start.

_____

_____

SCRIPTURE

"Because he turned his ear to me, I will call on him as long as I live. The cords of death entangled me, the anguish of the grave came over me; I was overcome by distress and sorrow. Then I called on the name of the LORD: 'LORD, save me!'"

— PSALM 116:2–4

"For he has not despised or scorned the suffering of the afflicted one; he has not hidden his face from him but has listened to his cry for help."

— PSALM 22:24

"Because of the LORD's great love we are not consumed, for his compassions never fail. They are new every morning; great is your faithfulness."

— LAMENTATIONS 3:22–23

God, there are times when I can't find words to cry out to You. This processing and trying to understand my pain feels overwhelming. The grief feels like a wave that could crash over me, taking me under with its force. Yet I cry out to You because I believe in You and Your words of comfort and healing. Help me see what I need to see, say what I need to say, and know You more deeply throughout this process. I trust that You will be there with me, sandpaper in hand, to shave down the sharp edges of my grief. Thank You that You are always listening and responding to me!

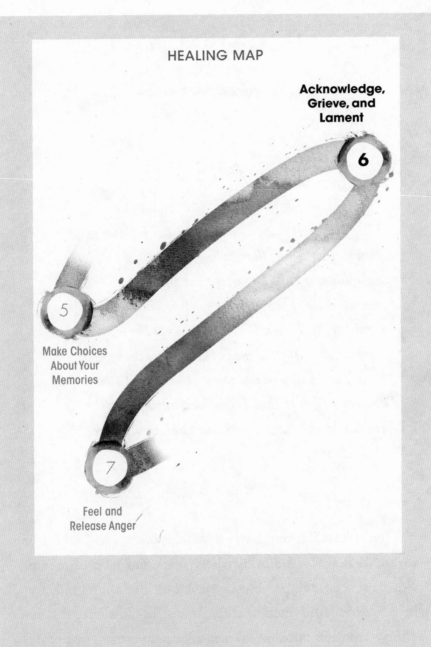

HEALING MAP

Acknowledge, Grieve, and Lament

6

5

Make Choices About Your Memories

7

Feel and Release Anger

Chapter 7

AT A BOIL

Writing the letter about anger that Michelle suggested is more challenging than I thought it would be. Here's the tension: if I'm 100 percent honest with my thoughts and words, they are not all God-honoring thoughts and words. When I filter, I don't know that I'm being 100 percent authentic. I'm conflicted. I'm not doing well with "not sinning in my anger." Do I put it all out there and repent later? Do I bring every thought captive and write something that I don't feel conviction or condemnation about?

— Sandi

The counseling couch was a familiar place. I had sat across from Michelle for months. Many tears and painful memories had been shared. Trust was being built. Progress was being made. And then, seemingly out of nowhere, this intrusive emotion bubbled up like a volcano during one of our counseling sessions. It was unfamiliar, shocking, and embarrassing to admit.

Anger.

I was angry. Deeply. Intensely. At people who had hurt me. At how unfair it all felt. And at myself.

We talked about past trauma. I was spewing out things like, "What kind of person does that? What gave them the right? I'm still so mad at them because they didn't simply hurt me then. They're still causing me pain today."

I remember Michelle saying, "I think we've discovered another root, Sandi. You're carrying around a lot of anger."

As difficult as it was to share my deepest emotions and hurts, it was even more challenging to acknowledge I had deep-seated anger. It hadn't defined my life (on the outside), but it was obviously a long-term tenant in my heart. Who wants to admit that? I didn't. I felt shame about it. I felt like a weak person for allowing anger to reside within me. It felt like failure to admit that something from decades ago was still stirring up such deep rage. I felt like a hypocritical Christian. How could love for God and intense anger both dwell within me?

I had acknowledged past pain. I had grieved the losses. Both were necessary and helpful. I think that is one of the reasons why anger surprised me. Why hadn't it gone away already? Why hadn't it dissipated over time? Why was anger still hanging around even after I had been processing through the pain?

More importantly, what should I do about it? How does anger get ushered out of your life?

Michelle suggested I write a letter and address it to

someone who hurt me. The letter would only be seen by Michelle and me. She explained it would be a way to acknowledge feelings, direct the anger where it needed to go, and then serve as a means of release.

The assignment sounded easy in her office. But as I began to put words to my feelings, I was shocked by the intensity of my thoughts. Words that had never exited my mouth were coming to my mind. I understood grieving through pain. But I had not encountered or acknowledged these newer emotions before.

I prayed. I asked God for freedom from the anger. I asked for help with the assignment. And I told Him I wanted to honor Him in the process. But I had no idea how to move forward.

The tension was real. I knew what I was feeling. But I felt like a horrible person. Only "bad" people get this angry. Only "bad" people think or say these kinds of words.

I felt like I had two options: (1) Be completely honest. Write the words. Embarrass myself. Ask for forgiveness later. Or (2): Filter. Write words that sound "better" and know I am not being honest.

Feeling stuck, I emailed Michelle. Here is some of her response:

> *I hear the tension of wanting to honor God in your thoughts and expressions, yet wanting to be honest in your humanity and feelings . . .*
>
> *The areas of sin I feel are most crucial to be aware of with anger are first, acting on it in a way that is*

harmful to others (a need for vengeance, even though the Lord says it's His), and second, suppressing it (pretending not to be angry at an act that has been a true violation of God's purity and righteousness, which turns to bitterness). Through the letter, I think we are trying to avoid either of these from occurring.

I am praying for clarity for you. God knows your heart and your mind to the depths—both your expression in humanity and your brokenness but also your heart for Him. I wonder if this is part of the process of surrendering all—anger, thoughts, emotions—to Him in honesty and from a place of hurt and sorrow.

Those words were so helpful and resonated as truth. I had no desire to harm or get even with anyone. And I didn't want to stuff or suppress my feelings any longer. I simply needed a way to acknowledge the anger.

With the guardrails for the letter defined, I sat down to write. The words flowed. They were honest but not sugar-coated. A few were not part of my normal vocabulary. I trusted that God knew my heart and that this exercise would be an important part of the healing process. I don't know if I sinned in my anger or not. I definitely felt guilty for the intensity of my emotions. I felt guilty for thinking and writing words that my kids would get punished for saying. I felt bad for directing the words and emotions toward someone else. And toward myself. None of it felt good. Was the Holy Spirit convicting me? Was the enemy condemning me? I wasn't sure. I humbly asked God to forgive me if I broke His heart as mine was healing. I believe He did.

The letter was emotional to write. For some reason, putting the words to paper stirred up a desire to scream. That may sound crazy and foreign (as it did to me). I felt like a water kettle that was whistling and screeching because it had reached its limit. The heat had to escape. So, I took the letter and sat in my parked car in the garage.

I read it. I cried. I screamed.

It felt like a release. It was a release.

Here is an edited (and G-rated) portion of the letter:

> *Writing this letter to you has been more difficult than I thought. Not because I don't know what to say. But because I feel like a horrible person saying or even thinking the things I want to say to you.*
>
> *Who gave you the right . . . to take advantage of a little girl? To take advantage of me?*
>
> *You were the darkest part of that dark room. Fear went through my mind and body that night because of you. Did it make you feel good to hurt me? You took my trust and trampled on me like I didn't matter. You made me feel worthless.*
>
> *I still want to throw up when I think about you.*
>
> *I want to scream at you so loudly that everything in me comes out . . . all of the rage and shame, the memories, the pain.*
>
> *This is my scream. It wasn't my fault. I didn't want you. You had no right! No right to make me feel small and used. Dirty and disgusting. Bad from the inside out.*

I'm angry that decades later I'm still angry. That's the real shame. You had no right to me that night. And you have no right to my life today. I'm turning on the light. And screaming for help.

Michelle asked me to read the completed letter during our next counseling session. And here's the interesting thing: I was expecting to feel the same heightened emotions that accompanied the writing. But I didn't. I was nervous, of course. There was a tear or two as I read. But the intense anger that had fueled the seething words before simply wasn't there. It had been replaced with calm and even contentment. The sense of peace was profound. Suppressed anger no longer had a grip on my heart. I felt lighter. Free from the heaviness. The anger had been heard. Understood. Redirected. And released.

The final step with the letter exercise, Michelle explained, was to dispose of the note. Burn it. Tear it up. Throw it away. I could choose. It was to be a symbolic ending. A final goodbye. She asked if I was ready to take that step.

I wasn't. The thought of throwing away the letter brought some anxiety. The freedom I felt from anger was real and profound. And so was the concept of finality. I simply needed a little more time with the letter.

In the days that followed I read it daily. Over and over. I'm not sure why. It didn't evoke a lot of emotion, but I felt a connection to it. It was a rendering of my soul. A reflection of deep pain. Words that I had felt for a long time but had only recently spoken. It was cathartic to me. It didn't feel right to rush past it. So, I didn't.

In time, though, I found myself reading the letter less often. Needing to connect with it less. During one of our counseling sessions, I shared that I was finally ready to let it go. With little fanfare, I simply threw it away. Again, I expected to feel something as I tossed it in the trash can. But I didn't. I had already "felt the feels." Released the rage. Made room for peace. The proof was in the trash.

UNPACKING THE PROCESS
WITH DR. MICHELLE

Recognizing and Releasing Your Anger

Are you carrying around anger? Are you ready to acknowledge it for what it is? Hear it out? Validate the wrong? Cry? Scream? Release its grip on you?

We're very good at thinking about anger and how or whether it should be in our lives. How or whether we express it. How we use it. Whether or not it's productive. But usually, we don't give ourselves a whole lot of latitude to feel it or show it. We think that the only "good" anger is the righteous anger we feel when someone has wronged God. The flipping-tables-in-defense-of-God-and-His-people kind of ire. A young child abused by those who should have protected and loved him . . . a social injustice that goes on and on for generations . . . an innocent life taken. In circumstances like these, we feel justified in letting our emotions rage.

Other times, our anger isn't quite as noble. Irritation at a neighbor's barking dog, indignation at a traffic ticket, that ugly spat with our spouse—they're not our finest moments. But the reality is that we're human. We all get angry. For reasons justifiable or not. Repeat after me: "I am angry at times." And that's okay. The key is to acknowledge that anger. To permit ourselves to feel it. To consider what we do with that anger.

You may also feel angry at God, mad at other Christians, or perhaps a church that hurt you or abandoned you in your time of need. These often are the most painful experiences of anger, as they are directed at those who were our safe landing places. Perhaps you are angry because it felt, in your experience, that God, other Christians, or the church did not show up for you at the right time to prevent the thing from happening (or to help you heal from it afterward). Perhaps it feels like God has left you to your misery—like Job's wife who said, "Curse God and die" (Job 2:9). That may feel extreme to you, or you may be thinking, *Yep, I've been there too!* We must understand that Job's wife uttered that response out of a core of unbearable pain. Our pain and anger, which have to be directed toward someone or something, often land on God. This is part of the human story! But, in our pain, we miss the mark. It makes no sense to hate the good God, the perfect Father who promises (and delivers) compassion, grace, patience, faithfulness, mercy, and forgiveness.

As you move through this chapter on anger, and especially if you hold deep anger at God, consider David Powlison's words in his book *Good and Angry*: "Anger at God . . . presents a wonderful opportunity for profound personal growth . . . Handled rightly, it is the royal road into the dark disorder of the human heart." Yes, anger can be a "dark disorder" and can be directed toward God, toward others, and often toward ourselves.

Our human anger comes in many sizes and shapes: mild (frustration), medium (bitterness), and large (rage). Sharp (violence) and fuzzy (passive-aggressiveness). It can be a sour taste in the mouth or a volcanic eruption. Some of us display anger in our strong-willed or argumentative personalities. Others of us have internalized the anger to the point of bitterness and resentment. And if you're like me, you might seem calm and dormant on the surface, but in reality, you may have detached yourself from the emotion of anger because no one told you it was okay to feel and express it. You've stuffed it so far down that it doesn't seem accessible anymore.

In these cases, our go-to expression of anger may be the silent treatment while we get our emotions back under control. Or maybe our therapist taught us how to punch a pillow (and that works for the moment). Perhaps there's some slamming of doors. Or spending time in the pit of self-pity when we've been wronged. You can spend some time at the pity party; just make sure you're not overstaying your welcome.

The challenge lies in making sure our anger—and our expression of and response to that anger—is productive. That it has a purpose. That you may resolve the anger sufficiently to find peace, forgiveness, mercy. It can be constructive anger. If not, anger can become a dark, turbulent, life-destroying emotion. This is destructive anger.

How did I believe that Sandi's anger could be constructive (even though she wasn't an angry person) and that the expression of it could be life-giving? First, I knew she had truly been wronged by another human. As we are made in the image of God, when we are sinned against by another, it's simply inexcusable. Her anger was justifiable. But she needed expression of and ownership over her emotions and reactions before she could feel peace.

Second, it showed that she cared enough about her younger self (and her current self) to feel this kind of strong emotion. Apathy is the antithesis of healing. Anger often comes when something or someone important to us is threatened—even a memory of yourself as a small child and how you should have been treated versus how you actually were treated.

Third, it was appropriate to take some sort of action with the anger. But this action was contained within the safety of her relationship with God and within the counseling space. You'll see I didn't recommend that Sandi show up at the person's house to confront him (of course), and she didn't even mail the letter off. The action was seeing her words on a page and releasing the deep emotions that were associated with this person.

Fourth, it was key to examine the motives behind Sandi's feelings and expression of anger. Was it to punish the person? Or to lament the wrongdoing and ask God for help resolving the anger? If we are moving toward vengeance, that's exactly when we should stop. No vengeance has ever satisfied the original wrongdoing.

Remember that God is also angry at what happened to you, the lies that were told, and the offenses that occurred. He gets angry first, and we just emulate Him when our anger comes from love. As Powlison notes, "God's anger is not unpredictable and mean-spirited. It's the product of love betrayed (when he's the one being done dirty) and of compassion for the victims of injustice (when others are the ones being hurt)." God treats all involved in equal measure—with justice and mercy, with love and corrective anger. However, He often exhibits anger differently than we do, and it's helpful to look at His correct version rather than simply giving into our own way of feeling and exercising this strongest of emotions. God's anger is clearly and consistently characterized by:

- A slowness to anger and a quickness to show mercy (see Psalm 145:8–9)
- Justice and fair-mindedness (see Psalm 10:14)
- Logic, with a clear cause and effect (see Deuteronomy 29:27–28)

This is quite the list to follow, especially when anger can feel so overwhelming. Anger is one of our most powerful human emotions. But it cannot reside in us for too long before becoming internally and externally destructive.

While resolving anger is quite a process in itself, it is entirely possible. As you move through recognizing and resolving your anger, consider the following pathway forward. You may also find it helpful to write your answers in a journal as you contemplate your way of feeling, distinguishing, and progressing through anger.

- *Identify your type of anger.* Are you trying to emulate God's slowness to anger, are you stuffing, or are you leading with a hot temper? If you are stuffing, give yourself permission to feel. Following the path set below will help you give yourself permission to identify and feel. If you are quick to anger, take a deep breath, and slow your roll. We are meant to be patient (or "long-tempered" as the Greek word describes God), even when we are in the right with our anger.

- *Identify the person at the center of the anger.* This might be another person, yourself, or God—or a combination of all three. What or who was wronged? Who or what did the wronging?

- *Identify the source that is causing the anger.* Why are you angry? What was violated? Was it a value, an ideal, a dream, an injustice, or some dignity?

- *Name the cause and effect.* This helps to bring the anger from a purely emotional experience to one where rationality also has a place—just like our Father, who is both emotional and logical! This is essentially naming the root of the anger: this particular event happened, and then this was the outcome.

- *Take action with your anger.* We are trying to prevent the anger from becoming deeply rooted in resentment and bitterness. I think this is why Ephesians 4:26 says, "In your anger, do not sin': Do not let the sun go down while you are still angry." A reminder to hurry up and move through your anger before it becomes sinful. For many of my clients, expressing anger verbally and receiving compassion in return has been healing. Others, like Sandi, have benefitted from writing a letter from a voice that has long been silent. Now, these actions won't completely wash away your anger; that may not be possible this side of Heaven. However, they will provide you relief, release, and a measure of peace. This is a realistic hope, one grounded in the reality of your suffering, yet with a renewed sense of inviting healing.

• *Allow space in your anger.* I can't tell you how many clients—especially women—have come to me saying, "But I'm not an angry person." That's a spot-on assessment: at our core, we are not made up of one huge blazing ball of fury. But when we dwell in the tent of anger, we often forget to make room for other possibilities: for gentleness, patience, mercy, justice, compassion, forgiveness. I know, easier said than done! However, you are not intended to be a vessel full of anger and wrath. Wrath is God's territory, and much of that was resolved when Jesus came with His bridge-building (rather than bridge-burning) mercy. You, as God's beloved, are also a vessel for all of these vital pieces too. Consider: in your vessel, how much anger do you want to hold? How much forgiveness? Is there space for showing mercy to those who don't deserve it? How might you ask God for His help in making space in your vessel?

The pain you have experienced has caused a fork in the road. The choice, when offended, is between the path of bitterness and resentment or the way of grace and mercy and freedom, as Sandi experienced—and as you can. When you work toward a place of grace in your anger, you are releasing yourself from the pain. You're actively working toward living out the image of God that is forgiveness and grace, even when the tears may not be wiped away completely or when your enemies won't be vanquished until the very last day. You are moving toward God rather than away, toward an honest faith, with a cry of belief rather than a bellow of rage.

You have had the opportunity to process through some aspects of your anger. Here, we ask you to continue to focus on it for further reflection and to dig deeper into your patterns of anger, keeping in mind the hopefulness of seeing God's compassion and grace in the middle of your journey.

How do you typically feel and express anger? What has been the outcome for you and others around you?

_____

_____

How have you attempted to manage your anger? What has been the outcome for you and others around you?

_____

_____

As you work on moving through your anger, what are the possible outcomes? How will working through your anger affect your relationship with God and others?

_____

_____

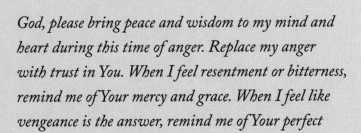

SCRIPTURE

"God is a righteous judge, a God who displays
his wrath every day."

— PSALM 7:11

"My dear brothers and sisters, take note of this:
Everyone should be quick to listen, slow to speak
and slow to become angry, because human
anger does not produce the righteousness that
God desires."

— JAMES 1:19–20

"For if, while we were God's enemies,
we were reconciled to him through the death of
his Son, how much more, having been reconciled,
shall we be saved through his life!"

— ROMANS 5:10

PRAYER

*God, please bring peace and wisdom to my mind and
heart during this time of anger. Replace my anger
with trust in You. When I feel resentment or bitterness,
remind me of Your mercy and grace. When I feel like
vengeance is the answer, remind me of Your perfect*

justice. Help me know Your purpose for my anger. May Your goodness and mercy follow me all the days of my life that I may dwell in the peaceful house of the Lord forever.

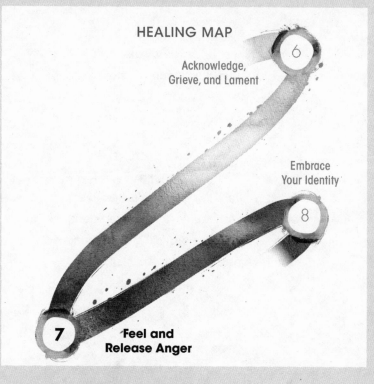

Chapter 8

PERCEPTION
IS REALITY

We had a good counseling session today. Michelle
affirmed that God is working and that we are
making progress. Praise God! I'm gaining insight.
Understanding the core issues. Recognizing negative
thoughts and challenging them with the truth more
often.

She asked me to pray about my identity—as a child
and as an adult today. What an assignment! I've
never thought about it. I know my roles: wife, mother,
Christian radio leader. But I think this exercise will
challenge me to go deeper. I'm going to ask God to reveal
truth as I ponder my identity.

– Sandi

It felt like the seasons were beginning to change.
Emotionally speaking, the first half—or more—of my counseling journey had felt like fall and winter. Change was slowly

happening on the inside, but it often felt like a tree losing its leaves. I felt exposed. Some cold realities had been revealed that had snowballed into what felt like zero-visibility conditions.

But now there were signs of fresh new growth. Hope was budding. This new season was all about learning to think in a new way that was rooted in truth rather than shame. And in learning to re-engage in relationships in a more authentic way. Over the next couple of chapters, we'll focus on restoring relationship with God and those closest to us. But in my counseling—and in this book—I was reminded that the starting point for all of that is with the relationship closest to us: the relationship we have with ourselves.

More specifically, the relationship I have with myself.

"What is your truthful identity?" Michelle asked me as we began this new chapter in my journey. It might be different than how I felt on any given day, she explained. Or how other people viewed me. Instead, our true identity is at the core of who we really are, and it affects everything else, which was something I hadn't understood or even considered before. It was a completely new concept. Through my counseling sessions I was now learning that this self-relationship directs each thought and decision in our lives.

It is the well that every other relationship draws from.

It was a stark reality to understand that my relationship with myself was in need of repair. Furthermore, there was no one else responsible for fixing it. Me, myself, and I were going to have to learn to own and change our relationship.

The assignment from Michelle was to consider my identity as a child and how it was similar to or different from my identity today. She explained that our identities change and grow as we do. I'm uncertain why that hit me so powerfully, but it did. It rang as true and good. Hopeful.

Before attempting to answer the identity questions, I prayed. I asked God to reveal the truth about how I saw myself as a child. How I saw myself today. And how He sees me today. Here is what I wrote:

Identity as a child

I felt ugly. Different. Bad. Unloved. Used. I felt like an unwanted mistake.

When I was in junior high school, I desperately wanted a relationship with God. I walked the aisle at church dozens of times. Or more. I had a sincere love for God but feared I was unwanted yet again. I desired to be loved by God. Hoped I was. But had doubt.

In high school I started drinking to excess. Drank with friends. Drank alone. Drank to get drunk. To get numb. Another secret kept.

As I consider my identity as a child, these words stand out: Secret keeper. Doubter (of God, self, and everyone).

Identity as an adult

The summer before my senior year of high school, my mom confronted me about the extent of my drinking and the lying to cover it up. She said, "Who are you? I don't know you anymore."

God used her words to pierce my heart. I gathered up all of the hidden alcohol in my room and car and drove out into the country. I smashed every bottle and cried out to God. I admitted that I didn't know who I was either. I surrendered the mess of my life to Him and asked for a fresh start. I stopped drinking. There was a newfound peace in my relationship with God. I became a truth seeker.

After getting married and having kids, my identity expanded to include a sacrificial, committed love for family.

Through a calling to serve in Christian radio, my identity grew again to include a heart for the lost. I was a truth speaker.

And yet there was another piece of me too: Perfectionist. People pleaser.

It was a stunning exercise. Before walking through this mental workout, I had never used most of those words to describe me. *Truth seeker. Truth speaker. Secret keeper. Doubter. People pleaser.* The disconnect was glaring. Truth in one hand and past shameful realities in the other. I was holding on to both.

Now I understood the importance of the assignment. Our thoughts (even the subconscious ones) steer every area of our lives. The words that summarized how I thought of myself, although never before spoken out loud, had been the backdrop of my deepest inner thoughts and emotions since childhood. Fuel for the fire that I never understood was burning, tainting, and shaping the way I interacted with my-self and everyone else. The filter through which I saw and experienced . . . everything.

It was jarring, but in a good way, because I was seeing and understanding the difference between truth and reality. The truth might be rooted in facts. But the reality of our thoughts—positive or negative, true or false—shapes who we are.

In the 1980s the political strategist Lee Atwater coined the phrase: "Perception is reality." In the world of politics, the premise is simple: what a voter believes to be true informs how they vote. So, as you can imagine, a politician's job often revolves around influencing the mindset and perceptions of voters. In the best of circumstances, it involves educating vot-ers. But for those less scrupulous, it can lead to manipulating voters by massaging or omitting facts.

There is something to be learned from this principle.

As believers, we understand the truth that our identity is rooted in Christ. We're His children, fully loved and embraced by Him, our heavenly Father. But I was now confronting the fact that our perceptions of who we are may be shaped (warped) by very real, very painful experiences in our past that conflict with the truth. Before I could fully embrace the truth of who God says I am, I needed to understand the root of my perceptions. Why? Because that was my present reality. It was the filter through which I saw myself and the world, even God's truth. And my past had been lying to me.

Something clicked for me. It was time to work on

re-engaging a relationship with myself that reflected the shifting perceptions in my mind and heart. My identity was changing—and I desired to have a truthful, compassionate relationship with myself. So, I went back to God with a new request. I laid at His feet all those words I had been using to describe myself for so many years, and I asked Him to tell me what He would say about me.

This is what the Lord brought to mind about my newfound identity: I was treasured by God.

It was unexpected. I had never considered that the God of the universe treasured me. I had always known He loved me. But I viewed it as an obligatory love: He loves everyone so He has to love me too. I don't think I ever said it out loud, but it was a deeply felt conviction rooted in shame, not the truth of God's Word. Yet there was now a deeper, more profound truth washing over my heart: God's love isn't rooted in obligation. His heart longs to be in relationship with me. And you.

God wanted meaningful connection with me. Okay, I was working on believing in that. But treasured me? That truth still felt clunky and foreign—too unbelievable to even consider. And yet . . . the more I prayed about it, the more determined I became to embrace it. To let it, for the first time, soak deep into my thirsty soul. It might take me a while to accept it fully, but I was realizing that God believed enough for the both of us. He was telling me how He felt. Had been telling me all along. And now that I was listening, I was hearing Him: I was no longer the unwanted one. The tolerated one. I was the treasured one.

God reminded me of a quilt my grandma had made. She had ten kids and a bazillion grandkids and great grandkids. But only one was born on her birthday. Me. So we celebrated together often. Perhaps that was one of the reasons why we had such a close relationship. She was approachable. Easy to love. And I felt special when I was with her.

I felt special the day she gave me the quilt too. It was made from scraps of material that she had around the house. There was no color scheme or pattern. No design. Just scraps, all hand sewn together with love. To some it would have qualified as a crazy quilt. Random, quirky, a mishap of material. To me, it was a treasure.

I'm not gonna lie. The quilt is not easy on the eye. It isn't pretty or impressive. It has no value in the marketplace. But it's one of the most beloved possessions I own. I have it stored away for safekeeping. A couple of times a year I take it out to see if it still smells like her house. If I can still hear her say, "Go ahead and cry, Sandi. You'll feel better." If I can still remember how I felt when we spent time together. That is why I treasure that quilt. It was not only a gift from her but a tangible reminder of our relationship as well. A treasure in my life.

For years, I thought of myself as that crazy quilt. Simple, quirky, mismatched. Of little to no value. But God has been challenging me to take another look, beyond the scraps and scrapes, and see the treasure.

Treasured. What a profound truth. What a tender way for God to reach my heart—to know I'm treasured by Him. Not because I'm impressive or do good things. Not because I look pretty or perform well. He loves me for me. He loves the time we spend together. He cherishes me. Thinks fondly of me.

Treasures me.

That was so challenging for a wounded heart to grasp. The pain and shame had convinced me that I was unwanted. That was my perception. But my healing heart was becoming aware of the truthful reality that I am beloved by my Father. Like a unique, handmade quilt. Still quirky, perhaps, but of priceless value. The psalmist had it exactly right: "You knit me together in my mother's womb. I praise you because I am . . . wonderfully made; your works are wonderful, I know that full well" (Psalm 139:13–14).

To know something full well, with heart and mind . . . That is congruency. It felt like a branding on my heart. A claim was made and accepted. I had known Jesus as Savior. But I was discovering Him as Abba Father. And He was making it clear I had a new identity, rooted in truth: "Sandi, you are treasured." That realization was a huge perspective shift for my mind and heart.

I am not broken. Unloved. Full of doubts. Keeping secrets.

I am treasured.

UNPACKING THE PROCESS
WITH DR. MICHELLE

Who You Really Are

Identity. Sandi's assignment was to describe her identity as a child and as an adult. As with many therapeutic homework assignments, it became much more as she considered not only who she was, but also where it all came from. The way she described herself was based on her early experiences . . . which then crept out into her identity as an adult, and even throughout how she thought God perceived her. Yes, she loved God and knew He *loved* her (in her mind, because He had to; that's what a good God does), but how could He possibly *like* her if all those harsh descriptors of hers were true? How could He treasure her?

According to the Oxford English Dictionary, the primary definition of identity is "the fact of being who or what a person or thing is." In psychology, and in Sandi's experience, identity is closely related to self-esteem, self-worth, and relationship with self—positive or negative. In his book *The Gift of Being Yourself,* David Benner defines identity as "who we experience ourselves to be—the 'I' each of us carries within." Identity also gives clues to others about who we are and what is contained in our life experiences. We can also carefully construct our identity to give us a sense of meaning, purpose, and even safety.

Identity is often described by the roles we play in life. For example:

- Daughter
- Mother
- Aunt
- Sister
- Wife
- Friend
- Student
- Employee
- Business owner

Those are all relatively neutral "I am" statements, right?

But here's where we get into trouble with our relationship with ourselves: when we start to assign negative descriptors to our identity. And even more so, when these negative descriptors become absolutes. When they follow "I am" statements . . . then we begin to believe and act out of these negative descriptors.

What are a few negative descriptors about our identity?

- I am not an intelligent person.
- I am a bad mother.
- I am a failed wife.
- I am a terrible friend.

These negative, absolute "I am" descriptors are sourced from two places: first, inside our own heads, and second, from the messages of others. When they come from an internal place, it may be that you've set an impossible standard for yourself.

There is little room for human mess-ups because that feels too out of control, too vulnerable, too weak, and therefore, unacceptable. When they come from the messages of others, that's when an old label is "re-sparked" by a current experience or interaction with someone else.

What's more, these two sources usually work annoyingly in concert with each other. Something sparks an old negative descriptor about your identity, which reinforces the internal perception, and on and on it goes. These negative "I am" descriptors only stand to keep us stuck, isolated, anxious, and even traumatized.

Look again at those examples of negative absolute identity descriptors. Can you begin to see the endless, destructive loop that this internal/external feedback can cause?

- *I am not an intelligent person.* (My family member said I was stupid and wouldn't amount to anything. Yesterday I failed a test, and that definitely means I'm not good enough to pursue a career I love.)

- *I am a bad mother.* (Someone once told me anger is bad. I yelled at my children because they were acting foolish. I was angry, and therefore I am a bad mom.)

- *I am a failed wife.* (A wife is supposed to meet her husband's needs, but abuse has made me uncomfortable with intimacy. Therefore, I've failed at fulfilling our marriage the way it's supposed to be.)

- *I am a terrible friend.* (My best friend died, and I didn't pray often enough for her to be healed. Therefore, I don't deserve to have a good friend.)

Let's revisit the Oxford English Dictionary definition of identity. The definition notes that identity is "the fact of being who or what a person or thing is." Oftentimes, as Sandi did, we get a message early on in our lives that somehow, somewhere along the way, turns into fact. Regardless of the truth, we believe it to our core. It becomes unassailable. Our reality. If that message was a negative one ... Well, you can see where that leads.

Sometimes the identity we had was a positive one, and then someone or some event—like a death or divorce—came along and blew it up. In the counseling room, I usually see this crash of identity happening when something threatens the way clients think about themselves. Often, it's when they have elevated one of their identities to a place of too great importance, identifying so closely with one particular role that it becomes the definition of who they are. When that identity is threatened or finds itself on unstable ground, it leads to self-doubt, negative thinking, and even depression and anxiety. You may be asking yourself questions similar to these:

When I got divorced, was I still a good wife?

When I was fired, was I meant to choose this career?

When my child bullied another, was I still a good mother?

We all have a core identity, a specific being, on which we set all our other identities. The danger here is that all of our identities outside the image of Jesus are fallible. They are ever-changing (depending on others' opinions as well as our own) and temporary (since we won't need roles in heaven). Not exactly what we want to set our lives upon!

Recently, I messed up with a client. It wasn't a life-endangering error, but I mixed up my calendar and missed an appointment. To relationships that are supposed to be built on consistency and trust, this was not a smooth move. True, it was an honest mistake, one that even the most attentive therapist has probably made at one point. But that mistake echoed around the cave of some old messages I didn't even know I was still carrying around. My thoughts went something like this:

You messed up.

You're bad at relationships.

Therefore, you're a bad therapist.

See how fast that can happen? These thoughts occurred at the speed of light and had the potential to dive-bomb my entire mood and interactions for the rest of the day, if not longer. If I let these feelings fester for very long, they could even convince me that I shouldn't even be a therapist anymore because I'm no good at it.

Can you see the power of the lie in that story? I had to pull myself out of the negative identity spiral by checking the facts in the story. What else was there to consider in addition to the absolutes above?

I messed up.

This is a mendable mistake.

*God will help me, and my client, recover from this
mistake when I apologize.*

*I am a good therapist because He helps me be a
good therapist.*

See the critical difference? What I told myself in the first
story was full of thin conclusions—i.e., a short, incomplete
story of my identity. The second story took into account the
fullness of the situation, without denying the mistake but including thick conclusions. It contained a different perspective,
theme, and even a new character in the story—God and His
descriptors over my work. This story reflected the truth of a
second chance and the fact that I am a helpful therapist—of
which there is much more evidence than the original story.
We're not talking about an ego boost just for the sake of feeling better about yourself. What we are talking about here is a
truthful change in thinking. To move from the negative, absolute "I am" statement to "Wait a hot minute, there's more to
the story."

You can imagine the different outcomes with this
re-storying.

Yeah, big deal, you may be thinking. *One missed counseling
appointment. What I've done is so much worse.* That kind of guilt
and condemnation only adds to the I'm-a-failure story of your
mistakes or identity. It becomes an echo chamber with the
mistake in the center. Even more, it suggests a level of worthi-
ness versus unworthiness.

Allow me to offer a gentle reminder: there are no degrees of "worse" in God's economy of grace. His love and

compassion come without restrictions or conditions. So, can you extend some of His grace to yourself today? The act of borrowing that grace is the first challenge to the story you've been telling yourself.

When Sandi and I met, it was clear she knew Jesus and had a relationship with Him. Knowing God's love was not the issue. But the pain of her past rejection and abandonment had led to a mental and emotional block that caused her to doubt God's like for her. Not His *love* for her, but His *like* for her. And if He didn't or couldn't like her, there was no way she could feel treasured by Him.

Maybe this is a core experience for you too.

We know God's love and forgiveness are deeper than we can ever comprehend. But what about acceptance and simply being liked by God (much less treasured!)? Don't we all just want to be liked, especially by the Creator of, well, everything? Being liked gives us the freedom to operate fully in a relationship, to be vulnerable, and to rest in a place of true identity.

I see this often in the precious women I meet in the counseling room. They know God loves them, just as He loves you. There's so much evidence of this in John 3:16, "For God so loved the world that he gave his one and only Son, that whoever believes in him shall not perish but have eternal life." I can see your eyes moving over those familiar words, your mouth speaking them quietly again. You believe His love to be true. You believe it because God declares it.

And yet, what if that love feels real but there's still some relational distance between you and God? What if, as with others in your life, there's this underlying fearfulness that He doesn't like you?

You may feel like your own past pain has created this veil of doubt. Maybe you feel like you've messed up too often to be liked by God. Perhaps you are convinced that He just forgives and loves you out of obligation. Perhaps you haven't been liked or appreciated in other relationships, and that's affecting your experience of intimacy with God. You may wish to protect your heart, even from God. If those fears are present, they can create a wall that prevents true intimacy with Him.

What are some of the indicators that there may not be the desired level of true intimacy between you and God? Take time to read through this list prayerfully, asking God to reveal if any of these ring true.

- *Discomfort with spending time with God.* When we spend a good amount of time with someone, we typically feel more known (at least more known than, for instance, the momentary relationship with the grocery clerk you see once a week or even your primary physician who knows your body but not your heart). Likewise, spending deep, intimate time with God can make us feel more seen, which makes us feel more vulnerable—both of which may be terrifying and good!

- *Engaging God through to-dos.* Yes, God calls us to serve Him, but too much emphasis on the service aspect of the relationship may mean that we are avoiding the intimate time spent sitting with and in Him. Perhaps there are old messages that you must do (and do well) to be liked. But that is not what qualifies a relationship with God. Step away from the unfinished list for a moment and remember: God created us to be human beings rather than human doings.

- *Ascribing characteristics to God that aren't His.* Our earthly parents, for better and for worse, teach us early on how to engage with God. So do our other relationships from childhood and right through to the present time as you read this. It's natural to learn and look for patterns in all of our relationships and to assume characteristics across the board. If you had a more distant parent, for example, you may see God as far-off, remote, disinterested. On the other hand, if you had a securely attached relationship with your parent, you probably feel God is a safe place to bring your needs, your sorrows, your joys. If your first friend betrayed you and talked behind your back, you may wonder how God could like you. If your husband declared one day that he no longer loved you, you may wonder how God could love you.

If any of these indicators apply to your relationship with God, there is hope. There is nothing you can do or experience that changes the fact that God not just loves you but likes you as well. He treasures you. Everything about you. What would it do to your relationship with Him to know—to truly believe—this? To know He values you just as you are? To accept He doesn't agree with all those early and current messages that you aren't worthy of friendship? Of love? Wouldn't it be freeing? You could operate openly within the love of God as His child and as Jesus's welcomed friend!

Can you allow your heart to rest in this new knowledge? Can you feel beloved, treasured, celebrated, liked because Jesus opens His heart and hands and offers this freely to you?

REFLECTION

Identity helps us know who we are, both within and outwardly. Yet it can become a source of negativity and pain all on its own. Loving God, but not accepting His appreciation and desire for a loving friendship with you, can be a barrier to an intimate relationship with Him and cause us to mistake our identity. Use the questions below to delve deeper into your thoughts and feelings around your identity and how you may begin to realign your perceptions with God's truthfulness about who you are.

Write a list of your current roles without assigning any descriptors (good, bad, etc.) to them.

_____

_____

Now, write what you most often tell yourself about your identity (using descriptors). What negative descriptors surface? Which neutral or positive descriptors are there? Given what you have read, how can you begin to challenge the negative descriptors?

_____

_____

Consider that God has made you for more than what others told you, what you've told yourself, and your mistakes. How does this change your identity?

_____

_____

What does God treasure about you? How would operating from this place of being liked, beloved, and treasured change the way you describe and relate to yourself? How would this assurance in your identity help you love others?

_____

_____

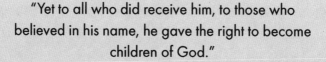

SCRIPTURE

"Yet to all who did receive him, to those who believed in his name, he gave the right to become children of God."

— JOHN 1:12

"He will take great delight in you; in his love he will no longer rebuke you, but will rejoice over you with singing."

— ZEPHANIAH 3:17

"Instead, I have called you friends, for everything that I learned from my Father I have made known to you."

— JOHN 15:15

PRAYER

God, I get so mixed up in what I tell myself—and what others tell me—about my identity. Some days it's positive, and many other days it's negative as I see my faults and failures so clearly. Help me see and reject these old ways of identifying that do not honor You and are destructive to the ways I'm thinking and feeling about myself. God, You said that I am more than my faults and failures, and that Your love goes on forever. Help me know that my identity is firmly rooted in that love and grace. Thank You that I can rest knowing that You tell me who I am. My identity is rooted in truth. Because You say so, I am treasured and liked too.

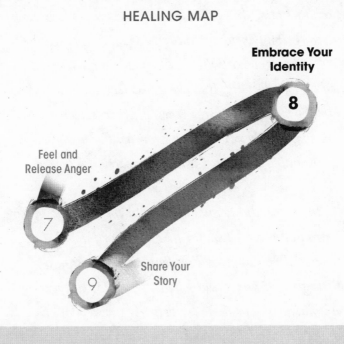

HEALING MAP

Embrace Your Identity

8

Feel and Release Anger

7

Share Your Story

9

Chapter 9

NAKED IN
THE STREET

*The conversation was scary. Especially at the beginning.
I felt exposed. My heart was racing. I clenched my
husband's arm and held on for dear life. I couldn't let go.
I couldn't talk. And I couldn't look at him. So, with eyes
closed, I simply held on and tried to catch my breath.*

*My heart was conflicted. On one hand, I wanted to
tell him everything. But I was also fearful. I have loved
him for more than thirty years. He is trustworthy. But
this was simply new territory for me. For my heart. As
irrational as it seems, I feared his reaction. I feared
his rejection.*

*The words didn't come easily, but the tears did. After
several minutes, I took the first awkward step. I shared
with Mike how I was disappointed and hurt as a
little girl. He knew that I had a strained relationship
with my dad. He knew I didn't like my stepdad. But
he didn't know the wounds I've been carrying around
or the messages I've been telling myself for years. He*

didn't know I hadn't liked myself. Or that my mind and emotions had been in conflict. I had never shared any of that with him. Until today.

The more I shared, the more fear seemed to lessen its grip. It was a first step toward fostering deeper intimacy and trust. Two things that I desire . . . but also fear.

Michelle called this a "vulnerable conversation." She said it is an important part of my healing journey and also necessary for fostering more trusting, intimate relationships with those I love.

God, please give me courage. This is really hard. And good.

– Sandi

I remember sitting in Michelle's office when she first introduced the idea of vulnerable conversations. The concept was simple. Share some of my past hurts and the healing journey with those closest to me. Be more open and honest with my feelings. It was an important part of the healing out loud process. I think she told me how beneficial it would be for my heart. How it would help with congruency in my mind, heart, and relationships. How it would foster trust, which was a long-standing struggle for me. How it was the next step in the healing journey.

And then she said, "I think you're ready."

It all made perfect sense. I totally understood the why. But the words that came out of my mouth were, "Michelle, that feels like you're asking me to get naked and walk across the street. I don't think I'm ready for that!"

We both laughed. But the sentiment was truthful. It felt like I was being asked to allow someone to see all of me. Completely exposed. I couldn't imagine a more vulnerable situation—except being stark naked and walking out into a busy street. In my mind, these two scenarios felt the same. I was scared to death of opening myself up and sharing my feelings and my past, even with my husband. It felt terrifying and risky. I had learned that vulnerability always ended in hurt or rejection.

She didn't realize it, but Michelle was trying to pop my bubble. I have often thought of my life as one being lived in a transparent bubble. Everyone can see me. Hear me. But no one can touch me. I'm on the inside of the bubble, and they're kept safely on the outside. I'm untouchable.

It's like hiding in plain sight. But no one really knows you're hiding. They think they know you. And to a degree, they do. But there is always a layer of protection between you. If they can't touch you, they can't hurt you—that is how transparent-bubble life works. That is how I have lived. How I liked it. And loathed it. I liked the protection or safety that the bubble gave. But I also recognized the loneliness it fostered. I knew I was missing out on a richness in relationships.

But vulnerability . . . That is another ball game. To me, vulnerability meant popping the bubble. Removing the barrier and the distance. Letting someone get in. Get close. Touch me. Know me intimately. I'd have to trust them fully. And that was scary. No one felt emotionally safe to me. It wasn't that they were unsafe. It was that I didn't have the confidence or security to be completely emotionally honest. I struggled with trust and vulnerability.

I wasn't completely walled off from my family or friends. They knew me quite well. We had meaningful relationships. But in my heart, I was holding back. I wasn't willing to be 100 percent vulnerable with giving or receiving in relationships. I feared someone discovering I wasn't as good as they thought. I didn't want them to view me as damaged. I feared being known. I feared being rejected. I was emotionally hiding. Which fueled more shame. That was the cycle. Wash. Rinse. Repeat.

Until I started to recognize it for what it was and chose a different path. And crossed the street.

Michelle and I talked a lot about vulnerability and the desire to be truthful and trusting with those closest to me. I told her I wanted to break the shameful cycle. I very much wanted to be known. I desired more openness and intimacy in my relationships; I simply didn't know how or where to start.

Michelle asked me to make a list of my internal motivations for vulnerability. Here were my reasons for wanting more vulnerable conversations and relationships:

- *God wired us for intimacy.* With Himself and with others. From the beginning of time, He has been building and restoring relationships with people and between people. He created the idea of relationship and intimacy. If I have an intimacy problem (which I do), then it will affect every relationship I have—with God and with everyone in my life. His desire for my life and relationships includes intimacy. I want the full extent of God's good plan for my life.

- *I want to be fully known and fully loved/accepted.* I don't want rejection or past hurts to define me. Or be the totality of what I feel. If I'm not fully known, then I will never be fully accepted. That will feed the incongruency that I've been living. Vulnerability is a step toward freedom.

- *It is life-giving. To me and others.* I believe vulnerability will usher in more fulfilling relationships for me to pour into and draw from. Those closest to me are worth investing in. They deserve it. I do as well.

- *I'm not damaged or bad, so it's okay if others get to know me.* There is no need to hide. I have less fear of rejection and judgment because I'm listening to truth more than shame. Fear will not define my relationships any longer. I will trust the truth of who they are and who I am.

- *It fosters trust.* I desire to grow in my ability to trust. I don't want to sabotage my relationships or rob either of us in those individual relationships from the fullness of being known and trusted.

Now I had my list in hand. But that didn't mean I was miraculously ready to embrace vulnerability. Why? Because vulnerability is hard. I'd been hurt. And to someone who has been hurt, vulnerable situations can cause feelings of distress. Opening myself up and being vulnerable was a trigger for all kinds of emotion and fear. It felt unsafe. Like pain and rejection were certain and just around the corner. It felt like my heart had a photographic memory with perfect recall of every time it had been bruised or broken. And with every invitation to be vulnerable came an internal alarm: *Warning! Danger ahead! Retreat to the bubble!*

I didn't want my heart to be broken again.

I didn't want someone else to see the brokenness in my heart that has been hidden away.

I didn't want to be rejected.

Vulnerable conversations require you to give something away. A piece of yourself. It may be a piece of your story. A memory. A private thought or desire. A fear. A dream. Something that has been safely tucked away.

I'd been tucking for decades. But now, I was going to have to open up and place my trust in someone and choose to share my hidden pieces. Who would be eager to put themselves in that kind of situation? Who would be willing to?

As it turned out, me. I was willing. It was terrifying. Painful. Exhausting. But I knew it was necessary. And worth it.

And it was. When you journey across the street, you see things from a new perspective. The work God ended up doing in my heart and in my relationships was life-giving to me. It also revealed I was not the only one affected by my choice to live in my emotional bubble for years. It had impacted every relationship, especially my marriage.

It would have been easy to justify and defend my self-protective behavior. At times, I'm sure that I did and still do. But recognizing, owning, and changing is part of the healing journey. Forgiveness is as well. I remember discussing forgiveness many times in a variety of contexts with Michelle. Forgiving people who hurt me. Forgiving whether someone asked for it or not. Forgiving myself.

But this time, I realized I needed to ask my husband to forgive me. I'm not sure that he had even realized I had been emotionally detached in our relationship. But I knew it. And I knew it wasn't good or fair to his heart. And I knew we needed to talk about it. Another vulnerable conversation. He didn't suggest it or require it. But I value his feelings. And it was good for my heart and soul to walk across this street. To ask for his forgiveness.

I recapped our conversation in my journal:

I have loved you for more than thirty years with a faithful, resilient, committed love. But I have also, to varying degrees, withheld and been guarded emotionally from you. I was not always aware of it or intentionally trying to hurt you. But I have hurt our relationship and our intimacy.

I have held on to an "I have to do it alone" mentality. I think alone. Process alone. Feel alone. Hurt all by myself. I have emotionally shut down and shut you out. I am sorry. Will you forgive me?

I don't want to live that way any longer. It isn't honoring to you, our marriage, or God. And it is a lonely way to live. I want to invite you into my thoughts, my emotions, my pain, and my joy. I want to share myself with you completely.

My husband responded very tenderly and graciously. He said several things that were very affirming and meaningful. He said he thinks my heart has always been available and accessible to give love away to him, to our kids, to hurting people, etc. But he thinks I struggle with making my heart available and accessible to receive love. He said he thinks I put walls up to protect myself because I've been hurt before—and he understands that. And he affirmed how much he and our kids love me. He said he sees my walls coming down.

What a gift. He knows me. And he loves me.

Talk about feeling all the feels! These vulnerable conversations run the full scope of emotions. Fear. Doubt. Courage. Humility. Surrender. Anticipation. Acceptance. Relief. Pure joy.

After several vulnerable conversations with my husband, I also crossed the street with my kids, my mom, and a couple of my best friends. Looking back on each of those encounters, I realized a few things:

- *Fear is a liar.* The fear I felt leading up to and through each of the conversations I had was very real. But not rooted in truth. Shame had magnified the fear to a point that it seemed believable and inevitable.

- *Popping the bubble pays off.* Popping the bubble was life-changing. It opened the door for even more vulnerable, honest conversations. To bare your soul with someone you trust and experience love, understanding, and acceptance in return is so life-giving!

- *It was me, not them.* I was loved before, during, and after each conversation. I realized they already loved me completely. I was the one who was holding back.

- *It gets easier to cross the street.* I didn't realize that practice was needed to be vulnerable. But it was. And the fear lessened each time. With each conversation also came experiential knowledge that there are people who desire to know you as much as you desire to be known.

- *It was worth the risk and the cost.* There is an ease and a freedom in my closest relationships that wasn't there before. I no longer fear sharing my feelings or being rejected. In a nutshell, God used these vulnerable conversations in powerful ways with the people I love the most. It allowed me to move toward the right people emotionally, not away from them. What a gift. To everyone involved.

A vulnerable conversation, as I discovered, is a courageous gift that you are both giving and receiving. The words you share are a peek into your soul, which is a gift to anyone who loves you. The affirming words they give back to you are an unexpected offering to your soul. And it all starts when you speak the first word out loud.

Cranking Open the Valve

It was difficult for Sandi to see, at first, that being vulnerable was a brave step to take. I framed it as courage because it was emotionally risky, and it took a huge measure of strength to move forward with telling another. Professor and *New York Times* best-selling author Brené Brown describes it well: "Vulnerability sounds like truth and feels like courage."

Do you feel that little internal niggle (or the big ol' urge) to retreat from vulnerability? Try not to put this book down and walk away! It may be a reasonable survival instinct to feel and respond this way. But before you make any choice, can we take a look at what's going on behind the urge to retreat? To go back to the old, safe patterns?

Before you're ready to heal out loud, you may find that you're holding onto patterns of self-protection. At our core, we yearn to be seen, validated, and loved. But put-downs, hurts, trauma, and rejection muddy the emotional water. After those experiences, the desire to be known is at odds with the very real fear of being hurt or rejected again. So, instead of allowing people to know us fully, we may limit access to our hearts, which in theory, increases the likelihood of being accepted and limits rejection. This is the pattern of self-protection.

This protective pattern may play out in different ways for you. Consider which of these resonates with your heart:

- *Caring for others' feelings more than your own.* On the surface, this seems honorable and even Christlike. But the problem is this scenario doesn't honor everyone involved. It isn't Christlike to devalue anyone's feelings, including your own. Sandi didn't know how to honor and share her feelings while also not hurting and protecting someone else. A suffer-in-silence pattern emerged. Well-intended, but not rooted in honesty for everyone involved. You may have learned to hold and hide deep-rooted feelings and emotions and, somewhere along the line, to disregard them as unimportant. You want to protect others' hearts but aren't attending to your own.

- *Protecting yourself from rejection by walling off access to your heart.* When we've been wounded, we never want to find ourselves in vulnerable situations again. It may feel safer to keep your feelings, desires, fears, and emotions to yourself—so you're not "found out" as someone bad or needy. This is a natural human instinct for survival, but it severs the human connection that God so treasures.

- *Feeling like you're still in control.* I work with women all the time who feel anxious when the world feels out of control. (That's me, too, on many days). We're used to running the family schedule, keeping the plates spinning at work, and helping to manage the lives of those around us. Control helps us feel safe! But it can also be a pattern of self-protection, to our detriment. You may also want to control how people react to you, especially when you start to share the deepest, darkest stuff you have carried for so long. Giving up that control, ironically enough, is where you will find freedom and grace in relationships.

- *Avoiding pain.* Humans are built to avoid pain. When you walk into the edge of the countertop and bruise your hip, you are certainly going to avoid it in the future. For Sandi, her early experiences with relationships gave birth to pain avoidance, which then turned into vulnerability avoidance. In relationships, we can describe pain in a variety of ways: rejection, disappointment, shame. Are you settling for relational transactions rather than deep, meaningful relationships because you feel you can avoid potential pain?

When we tell our truthful story to another, we are not giving into the lies that our story is embarrassing, shameful, and unworthy to tell. We are rebelling against the message that shame sends to "sit down and be quiet." We are, in a sense, turning that directive back onto the pain and the shame and telling them to "be quiet, already!" Shame has taken away enough from us. Shame will tell us it is possible to avoid pain. This is a fallacy. If you've worked hard on re-establishing your relationship with yourself and your identity in God (remember, you are already beloved, treasured, and liked), you can begin to confront this lie. It takes courage to stand up, to find your legs, and to cross the street. To stage your quiet rebellion against the shame. But you and God can handle telling your story because you're not as afraid of pain and rejection anymore.

Frederick Buechner, a prolific author and theologian, explains it perfectly in his book *Telling Secrets*:

> *I have come to believe that by and large the human family all has the same secrets, which are both very telling and very important to tell. They are telling in the sense that they tell what is perhaps the central paradox of our condition—that what we hunger for perhaps, more than anything else, is to be known in our full humanness, and yet that is often just what we also fear more than anything else. It is important to tell at least from time to time the secret of who we truly and fully are even if we tell it only to ourselves—because otherwise, we run the risk of losing track of who we truly and fully are and, little by little, come to accept instead the highly edited version which we put forth in hope that the world will find it more acceptable than the real things. It is important to tell our secrets, too, because it makes it easier that way to see where we have been in our lives and where we are going. It also makes it easier for other people to tell us a secret or two of their own, and exchanges like that have a lot to do with what being a family is all about and what being human is all about.*

*Finally, I suspect that it is by entering that deep place
inside us where our secrets are kept that we come perhaps
closer than we do anywhere else to the One who, whether
we realize it or not, is of all our secrets the most telling
and the most precious we have to tell.*

When you open up and include another in your story, it
means you are no longer the secret keeper. No longer hiding parts of yourself in the dark. However, please know that
doesn't mean there is an expectation to throw open all of the
curtains to let the light in. Throwing the curtains open all at
once may leave you blinded, confused, and searching for safety
in the dark again. You have to take it slowly. Carefully. Sandi
and I took steps to ensure she wasn't blinded. We made sure
she wasn't walking across the street without looking both ways
first. Safety first, and then vulnerability second.

As you consider telling another your story, a few things to
keep in mind:

- *Pray, pray, pray.* Ask for the Holy Spirit's guidance
  as you step into this vulnerable place. If you need
  to revisit some of the chapters of this book before
  you go across the street, do so. This brave step needs
  God's hand and help.
- *Identify the trustworthy person (or people) you plan to
  speak with.* This person has a history of loving you
  well. They are empathetic. They have earned your
  trust. They may already know parts of your story. But
  here's the thing: someone has to take the first step

forward into the street. That's you, especially after reading this book and as you have been working toward your own sweet healing.

- *Do it at your own timing and pace.* Very few of us wouldn't pull a muscle trying to sprint for the first time since elementary school. However, we might be able to go for a longer distance if we jog first and warm up the relational muscles. It will take time. And that's okay. Vulnerability and trust weren't built in a day.

- *Perform a slow vulnerability experiment.* See what happens when you put bits of yourself out there. See how it is returned with love and care by others.

Here's a small way to start what I've used myself and have encouraged others to use: the next time someone asks you how you are, answer honestly (as honestly as you can). We are 100 percent conditioned to respond with an automatic "fine." Now, sometimes that's completely true. Sometimes we may even truthfully say, "Great!" because we found out we fit into last year's jeans or our kids got a nifty award or we just received an answer to a prayer.

But what about the other times? The times when we didn't get the dream job. When it seems God didn't show up in our prayer against an illness. When our kid got caught shoplifting. During these difficult times, when a caring friend or coworker asks, "How are you?" and life is just spit-miserable, why not answer them honestly? Because we assume, in our self-protectiveness, that they don't want to hear what we have to say. And we automatically shut the flow valve to vulnerability.

Next time, take them up on their offer to hear how you're doing.

Awhile back, my pastor asked how I was doing. First instinct: "Fine! Great! Fabulous!" even though a small bit of my world had just crashed and was aflame right in front of my eyes. I didn't want to take time out of his busy day or be a complainer or, honestly, to feel even more vulnerable at that moment. Shame whispered that he wasn't really interested in anything but a positive response. Shame whispered that it wasn't worth the time to explain it.

I resisted the temptation to protect my feelings (and give in to the shame) and responded, "Actually, I'm feeling super discouraged."

What I received from my response, without even needing to ask, was comfort and empathy and just a moment of being truly seen. My pastor acknowledged my feelings and offered some comforting words. He put aside what he was busy with and simply listened. And then we went on with our respective days. The crash site was still a crash site, but the flames had been extinguished enough to become manageable.

Try an honest answer, and see how it is returned. You can't exercise your vulnerability muscle without stretching it first. Here is what Ecclesiastes 4:9–10 says about relationships as we work together (and this includes the hard work of healing): "Two are better than one, because they have a good return for their labor: If either of them falls down, one can help the other up. But pity anyone who falls and has no one to help them up."

Conversely, in the verses shortly before these, the writer of Ecclesiastes describes a person who, devoid of companionship, becomes bitter, isolated, discouraged, and discontent. Yikes! You don't want that, do you?

A healing out loud process is messy. It's challenging on the heart and mind. However, as in this verse, our most vulnerable time of falling can reap a "good return" when we allow someone alongside to help us up. The good return, as Sandi experienced, can be a deepening of a relationship, and within that relationship, moving about with more ease and freedom to be who God calls us to be. After all, one of God's defining characteristics is His desire to be relational, within us and among us. He does not want us to be isolated, with walls of secrecy built around us. God desires us to see and feel His presence in our relationships with Him. We can be more courageous in our vulnerability because we know God is with us, always.

REFLECTION

What a step we have asked you to take! To see God's presence in places you may have not before. To recognize His presence can give you courage. To allow this courage to carry over into being vulnerable in your relationships. As you ponder the next step for yourself, consider these reflections as you continue to walk forward into healing—and maybe even across the street!

What does it mean to you to "get naked and walk across the street"?

_____

_____

Identify one or two trusted people with whom to share the story that you've been working so hard on during this book. How might you approach them? How do you think they will respond?

_____

_____

When shame tries to shut down the vulnerability valve, how might you put on bravery and do it anyway? How does God's presence make you braver?

_____

_____

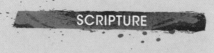

"The LORD is with me;
I will not be afraid."

— Psalm 118:6

"My intercessor is my friend
as my eyes pour out tears to God;
on behalf of a man he pleads with God as one
pleads for a friend."

— Job 16:20–21

"He heals the brokenhearted
and binds up their wounds."

— Psalm 147:3

"There is a time for everything, and a season for
every activity under the heavens: a time to be
born and a time to die, a time to plant and a time
to uproot, a time to kill and a time to heal, a time
to tear down and a time to build, a time to weep
and a time to laugh, a time to mourn and a time
to dance, a time to scatter stones and a time to
gather them, a time to embrace and a time to
refrain from embracing, a time to search and a
time to give up, a time to keep and a time to throw
away, a time to tear and a time to mend, a time to
be silent and a time to speak, a time to love and a
time to hate, a time for war and a time for peace."

— Ecclesiastes 3:1–8

PRAYER

God, I often don't feel brave, especially when it comes to being vulnerable. You have seen how I have been wounded in the past by others, and this pain feels so big sometimes. I see that the pain, the distrust, the rejection, have only served to put a barrier between me and others. Yet, God, You desire for us to be in deep relationship with one another and with You. You say healing can occur by You, through others. Show me how this is possible! I ask that You show me the way to walk across the street. Be with me as I take this step.

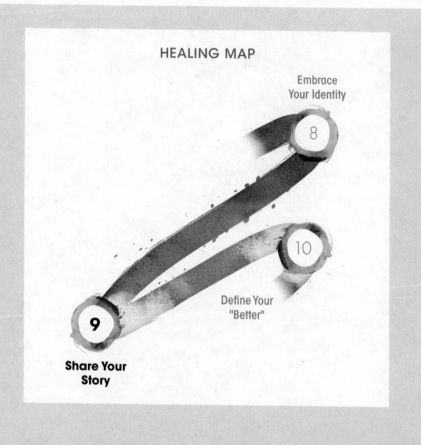

HEALING MAP

Embrace
Your Identity

8

10

Define Your
"Better"

9

Share Your
Story

Chapter 10

LESS YUCK

We talked about getting better today in counseling. I told Michelle that some days I feel better. Other days, I still wrestle with negative thoughts. I asked how I will know if I'm getting better? Michelle said, "Better isn't the absence of 'yuck.' It is knowing how to navigate through conflicting thoughts and feelings in an honest way." That made me feel . . . better!

– Sandi

I know that "yuck" happens. (I've seen the bumper stickers.) But I'd noticed I was recognizing and challenging yucky self-condemning thoughts more quickly. I was having more truthful conversations with myself and others. The weighty sadness and grief were lifting. And a couple of friends (unprompted) told me I seemed more lighthearted. All signs of better!

Funny thing, both Michelle and Mike used the word yuck when talking about me getting better. Mike said my journey has been similar to the opening and prepping of our pool each summer. "You're working hard at finding balance, Sandi. You've dealt with all of the yuck that was hidden until the cover came off. Now, I can tell that things are getting clearer for you each day and you're seeing that it's safe to invite people in. We're all in the pool together, and you're becoming who you are intended to be." I never knew that being compared to our algae-infused pool opening would feel so good. When your husband and counselor both say there's less yuck in your life, I think you're getting better!

For me, it felt like the volume knob was turned down on the past shameful messages. I was leaning into and listening to truth more often—which led to more honest, compassionate conversations with myself and others. And there was a growing belief that I was actually okay. With myself. I felt more content and peaceful inside.

I couldn't wait to ask Michelle if she could see continued evidence of progress as well. I should have known better than to ask a counselor such a question. She responded with, "What changes are you seeing, Sandi? Oh, and by the way, I like your makeup. I've not seen you wear it before. Is that something new?"

I had to laugh at the skillful way she both avoided, yet still answered, my question. I had not worn makeup to any of our counseling sessions over the past year. In fact, when I first walked into Michelle's office, I was fifty-two years old and had only worn makeup a handful of times in my life. I didn't own makeup. Didn't know how to apply it. I had no issue with those who wore it. But I couldn't bring myself to use it.

During the counseling journey, we discovered that my reasons for not wearing makeup had nothing to do with makeup itself. Instead, my reluctance was rooted in two subconscious shameful thoughts: (1) I wasn't pretty and (2) I didn't want to do anything that could attract the wrong kind of attention. In other words, self-blame for past abuse.

So, the day I walked into the cosmetics department at Dillard's, sat down in a chair (sweating profusely), and asked the young lady for help was a big deal. It had very little to do with makeup and everything to do with getting better and tasting freedom. It also cost me an arm and a leg because I bought every product the young lady worked with. Why? Well, because I needed it all—I had no makeup at home. And because when I looked in the mirror she held up, I liked the way my eyes looked.

When I shared that story with Michelle, she said, "That is the first time I've heard you say you like something about yourself, Sandi. That is a great start!"

Evidence of better.

Around that time, I was in church (with makeup on), and our pastor shared the scripture that explains the armor of God (see Ephesians 6:10–18). I don't remember the exact words spoken, but I do know what I heard: *What if life is always a bit messy and a bit of a battle? It is. So, we need to be battle ready.*

It hit me: what if some of the battles we face in life are "out there" beyond our control? And what if some of them are inside of us? For the first time, I realized my mind was a battleground. And I didn't want to hand my thought life over to the enemy. I didn't want to buy into his lies any longer. And I didn't want to allow him to rob me of any more freedom. That sermon was the perfect timely reminder that this journey of mine wasn't a cure for the yuck but rather an equipping for the battle.

I was energized by the invitation to join in the fight. I remembered Michelle's question (in chapter four): *What would it look like for you to fight for yourself today?* I didn't have an answer then. But I did now. I would see myself as one worth fighting for. And I would grasp every weapon available to me for the ongoing battle. The first piece of armor mentioned in Ephesians is the belt of truth. The truth of who God is and who we are—powerful weapons for battle. And better was worth fighting for.

When I shared this aha moment with Michelle, she smiled. "Sandi, can you see it? You're not only fighting for yourself now, but you've also realized that you're not the enemy. You're not fighting with yourself any longer." I saw this renewed fighting spirit as further evidence of better.

During one of our final counseling sessions, I asked Michelle if she had ever noticed the scar on my right index finger. More than thirty years ago, I'd been washing dishes when I inserted my right hand into a glass. A glass glass. It broke, cut my finger, and severed a tendon. Surgery repaired the injury and gave me full mobility in my finger again. It is better. But a scar remains. Most days, I never think about it. The only time it comes to mind is when I inadvertently bump it and feel the zinging discomfort from the damaged nerves. I told Michelle that my scarred finger is more sensitive than the other unaffected fingers on my hand. It is healed. Out of mind. Functioning well. Better. But still hypersensitive when bumped.

That is how I feel about myself and my journey. I see evidence of healing, and I am still sensitive to bumps and pain. More susceptible to reacting to triggers that may not faze someone else at all. I don't necessarily like it, but it's true of my injured finger and of my wounded, but healing, heart.

I shared this with Michelle because as I pondered the evidence of better in my life, I thought about my scars. Some on the inside, others on the outside. But every scar is evidence of the injury, the healing, and the remaining sensitivities. Some days I feel the sting of the wound. Other days I don't think about it at all. And on the best days, I thank God for the visible evidence of His healing in my life.

Long after our counseling relationship ended and our friendship began, Michelle and I were having a lighthearted conversation. Everything about it was normal and good. Until it wasn't. I don't remember all of the details, but as we talked, we gradually moved into deeper emotional waters. I could sense something beginning to rise up inside of me. Some old feelings were triggered, and I didn't know what to do with them. Instead of trying to explain what I was feeling and wrestling with, I lashed out at Michelle and said, "Don't get all counselor-y on me."

I will never forget the look on her face. A mixture of compassion and confusion. She had no idea I was struggling emotionally—until I blurted out something I immediately regretted.

I felt horrible, and I'm pretty sure she did too. Later that day, after reflecting on what had happened and sorting through the emotions, I reached out to apologize. I told Michelle I was sorry for hurting her feelings. I shared that while we were talking earlier, I'd had some conflicting emotions circling around in my mind, and I got all tangled up in them. And instead of admitting I was struggling, I pushed her away with a verbal jab. An old self-protective habit.

She graciously accepted the apology and suggested a tactic for the next time this might occur. Because she knew it would. She recommended a code word for any time I felt caught in an emotional tornado. "How about 'tangled'?" she asked. She then suggested that if I was ever unable to or not ready to talk about whatever emotions were circling within me, I could simply say the code word. It would be an easy go-to for me and her cue to give me some time and space to process.

Even on better days, triggers seem to come out of nowhere, and they never seem to give fair warning. No siren or alarm goes off announcing the return of old shameful thoughts and feelings. In an instant, I can go from calm to calamity inside my mind. I've experienced it, even after the counseling journey ended. Triggers happen. Short-lived setbacks occur. Michelle said it's a normal part of life and the ongoing healing journey.

As Michelle and I discussed triggers and ongoing strategies, it occurred to me that every time I encounter a trigger, I have a choice to make: will I lean or will I lead? For me, the easiest but also most counterproductive option is to lean into the active emotion and shame. Give into the condemning thoughts. A friend of mine calls this "holding hands" with negative thoughts. The image is powerful: an unexpected condemning thought gets whispered into your ear. It's hurtful, and you know it isn't truthful or good for you. Do you lean in and hold hands with it?

No. It isn't your friend.

Instead, I'm learning to recognize the moment for what it is. An opportunity to lead my thoughts away from the tangle. I try to begin a conversation with myself, sometimes out loud, that centers around truth: I am not alone. God is with me. He treasures me.

I've discovered it is easier said than done. But it does get easier the more I practice. The more I lead. Sometimes I get it right. Sometimes I don't. I'm trying to give grace to myself when I lean a little too long. And celebrate the times that I choose to lead. It feels better!

UNPACKING THE PROCESS
WITH DR. MICHELLE

Diffusing Triggers and Moving Forward

I hear this check-in question often: "Michelle, how do you think I'm doing so far?" Behind this question is such hopefulness, and rightfully so. "Am I getting better?" means, "Please tell me all of this hard work isn't for nothing!" This is both a rewarding and, at times, a challenging question to respond to—not because there isn't progress, but because it's not a black-and-white answer!

While training to be a counselor, one of my classes included a group project. We were required to come up with a name, and we landed on "WIPs," standing for "Works in Progress." It was our way of acknowledging we were still early on in developing the skills necessary to be good counselors. We were humble and open to learning, seeing a lifetime ahead of understanding how to help other humans improve their lives. We also wanted to make sure that our work—the first word in the acronym—was included too. Our work needed to be recognized. We were striving. We were doing the assignments. (We were also trying to earn As.)

That's where I land when this question—"How am I doing so far?"—comes up in the counseling room. A work in progress. A balance of encouragement for all of the tools adopted and used, all of the insight developed, and all of the changes in relationships. Yet, there is also a truthful recognition that it is still "in progress." And oftentimes, that "in progress" is a part of the growth that sparks triggers and the resulting doubts. While we recognize it's normal to be in progress, it doesn't mean we sit back. (Who says, "I've arrived!" unless you're standing on top of Mount Everest? You still have to navigate back down!) We can continue our progress onward. So, let's take a moment to unpack and deal with one of the most difficult parts of "what's better": the triggers.

A trigger is a response from the brain that says, "Hey, do

you remember this?" Triggers come in all shapes and sizes, and can be both positive and negative. Oftentimes when we talk about them in counseling, they are framed from the negative perspective, due to a painful or traumatic experience. These kinds of triggers are followed by intrusive thoughts, anxiety, emotional numbing, feeling overwhelmed, and maybe even some dissociation. Dissociation is the brain's protection against trauma, in which we mentally go "somewhere else."

A trigger can be a visual or a scent, a piece of clothing or a place where something happened, a song or a sound or a voice, or even a taste that awakens a traumatic memory. Many times, the trigger is unknown until it's known—otherwise, we'd all be experts at routing ourselves around the potential trigger! The unknown (at least until it is identified) is one of the most difficult parts of triggers. They feel like they jump out of the dark, suddenly disarming the illuminating flashlight and protective pepper spray that we have entered the scary room with. And it may even happen on a perfectly sunny day. Or, as Sandi experienced, in a (seemingly) nonthreatening conversation with her therapist and friend.

As I noted, we all experience memory triggers, both good and bad (and everything in between). Hear me say, these triggers exist to protect us, not to heap harm back on us. Triggers are utterly normal and functional. During a traumatic experience, the body and mind take in everything that is occurring through all of the senses—whether we know it or not—and store it up for future reference. If the original situation was threatening, when what feels like a similar situation occurs, the body and mind are going to put the pieces together and scream, "Get the heck out of there!" Or, "Freeze up and no one will see you!" Or even, "Punch someone in the face!" (Hopefully not the last one, but it is a normal reaction.)

What you can see here, I hope, is that the body and mind are fully bent on survival. We sense a threat, and we respond to it. God, amazingly and faithfully, has given us this ability, even when—I know—it feels like a bit much (or a lot much). It's not always easy to handle. The survival instinct, when it reacts so strongly, can seriously get in the way of living your everyday life, in both minor and major ways. I understand, because I have also experienced myriad triggers over the years.

My father, like many men his age, consistently wore blue-and-white New Balance tennis shoes. After a long struggle with heart disease, Dad suddenly died from cardiac arrest in 2015. From that day on, my world has seemed overwhelmingly populated with men in their sixties wearing the same tennis shoes. These shoes are everywhere! At the airport. In the grocery store's cereal aisle. Strolling along at the park. One day, a client of mine came sauntering nonchalantly into the office with them on, causing me to step away, take a deep breath, and try to refocus as quickly as I could.

Every time I see these kinds of shoes, I am taken back, sadly, to the deep sense of loss I experienced with the passing of my father. Two days after he died, I drove his truck back from the garage where he'd been working to bring an old car back to life. In the passenger seat next to me sat his extra set of New Balance tennis shoes. I remember exactly how they were positioned, how clean they were, and remember wondering what was going to happen to those bright-white and navy-blue leather shoes.

Seeing similar shoes on father-aged guys in public is my trigger back to that moment. Slowly, this trigger is moving to the realm of affectionate memories that come from having a dad who loved a particular kind of tennies. New Balance shoes are my grief trigger. (Sounds weird, right? But that's the definition of a trigger—something unexpected, and yet, meaningful.)

While there are common types of triggers (visual, sound, place, smell), your triggers are unique to your painful experiences. Take a deep breath and consider: when you feel most anxious, sad, or unsafe (either by yourself or in relationship with others), are you triggered back to an earlier painful time? What pressed your trigger button?

The good news is we can identify our triggers and work with them—rather than against them—to decrease their effects on us. It may be hard to comprehend at the moment, but truly, God has given us these triggers for our protection and survival. The more challenging news is we shouldn't let them rule over us. Intervening between ourselves and our triggers means not automatically responding with anxiety, fear, or panic.

There are several ways to decrease a trigger's impact that have been wonderfully effective for my clients. I offer this short list as a place to begin. As you look over it, and as you discover your protective reactions to triggers, keep in mind that they are often deeply seated in our memories and it will take time to lessen your response. Be patient while you try these techniques, and make sure you try them more than once. Also, consider that if you choose a few that appeal to you the most, you can match a particular tool with your type of trigger (for example, turning on your favorite music in response to an auditory trigger).

- *Breathe deeply.* Start from the bottom of your diaphragm, fill your lungs, and exhale slowly. Inhale for five seconds and release for five seconds. When triggered, we breathe from the very top of our chests, reinforcing the fight, flee, or freeze mode that the body uses to respond to a threat. Breathing deeply tells the body there is no threat.

- *Validate what's happening.* Know there is nothing wrong with you. Triggers come as a natural response to a past hurtful or traumatic experience. You are coping, and working through the memories is the path to healing. Remind yourself of that.

- *Repeat a comforting scripture or phrase.* I often tell my clients who suffer from panic attacks to verbally repeat, "I am not dying." Even though it can feel very much like you're about to see Jesus face-to-face imminently during a panic attack, more than likely this is not true. Have an encouraging, strength-filled reminder scripture written out and pasted where you can see it, especially in a place where you are more likely to be triggered.

- *Change your mind.* Two of my favorite scriptures encourage us to (1) take every thought captive (see 2 Corinthians 10:5) and (2) think about noble, right, pure, lovely, admirable things (see Philippians 4:8). I bet you are not automatically dwelling in this place when you are triggered. But the encouragement is not that we *should* but that we *can* take every thought back from the triggered place. Find a thought of gratitude, of goodness, of a smile from a loved one, of a scrap of a hymn, and repeat it. Breathe, hold the thought for at least ten seconds, and notice the difference in your body's reaction and your emotions to these better thoughts.

- *Ground yourself.* One of my favorite exercises to do with clients is The Five Senses, which I mentioned in chapter five. God gave us our senses for a reason —to experience the world around us fully (and also to smell and taste bacon)—and we can use these handy tools to calm our bodies and minds. Start with five things you can see, four things you can feel, three things you can hear, two things you can smell, and one thing you can taste. Pause and focus on each sense, noticing, for example, the texture of the chair you're sitting in. Is it rough? Is it smooth? Is there a spot of baby food stuck on it? This will remove you from your memory and ground you to the present time.

- *Find a safe person.* This is where your work in "getting naked and crossing the street" comes in handy.

You've already identified a safe person, and they know part of your story. You can simply text them, call them, or as Sandi and I did, come up with a code word that indicates you just need to let someone know you've been triggered. Consider using the trigger code word like Sandi and I did—as a shortcut to explain yourself without having to go into detail. Amazingly, this will automatically calm your survival mode. You recognize that you don't have to do it alone.

- *Find a safe place.* One of the quickest ways to reduce the amount of time in a trigger is to feel physically safe. That may mean crawling under a weighted blanket for a few minutes. It may include taking a break by yourself in the bathroom. Or taking a walk—an incredibly effective way to be out in God's creation and let the adrenaline flow back to a regulated level. If you can't go anywhere at that moment, create a safe space in your mind using a detailed visual. That old technique of finding a happy place in your mind is wonderfully effective!

As we have now normalized for you, this process of working out "better" takes both time and effort. But in all of my work as a therapist, I have not seen one client who has not defined and reached a better place for herself when she devoted her heart, body, and soul to the work of healing and invited God into the process. That's not due to some magical therapeutic ability but God's great promise of showing up and doing His work of healing.

I know you want a timeline of when you'll get to the point of nonsuffering. I can't tell you how long it will take. I can't tell you how many tears you will cry—or will have cried—throughout your lovely devotion to working through this book. I can't tell you exactly what your "better" looks like.

I can tell you something about a three-legged stool.

Sandi asked me one day how I knew she was getting better, how she was healing from the past and moving forward into getting untangled. I often receive this question from clients. They desire reassurance from my viewpoint that they are making progress, both as a person external to them and as a professional in the brain business. I always give an honest response. Yet at the same time, the healing process is so unique to each person, and the changes are often so subtle (yet the impact so big) and so internally felt that it can be a great challenge to find the words to respond to this check-in.

I am sure Sandi thought I was off my rocker (sorry), but I used the illustration of a three-legged stool to provide a little definition around the healing process. If one of the legs of a stool is missing or shorter than the other, I explained, it's awfully hard to sit on it without it tipping over. All three legs are equally important. But when you have all three legs and they're all in equal length and stability, you can take the stool with you wherever you go and use it again and again.

So, what are the three legs that indicate healing?

1. You are naming your pain and speaking to yourself more gently, honoring and validating your experiences. You are also healing out loud by telling your story to others.

2. You are valuing yourself enough to take care of yourself patiently, in all of the realms that God has given you—relationally, physically, mentally, emotionally, spiritually—as best as you can.

3. You are opening yourself up to a new kind of vulnerable, sweet, intimate relationship with others, including your trusted relationship and friendship with God. And I'll bet others are noticing the changes in the way you are engaging in relationships, right?

Of course, after I shared the three-legged stool analogy with Sandi, I flipped the age-old therapist question right back to her: "So where do you think you are?" (We do that not to be snarky but because the client's answer is actually far more important to the healing process than our answer.) I ask you to consider the same question as you faithfully make your way toward the end of this book and reflect on your healing journey.

How's your three-legged stool coming along?

REFLECTION

Getting better is often a complicated process, full of memories, triggers, and times where you will wonder when it will all come to fruition. Although there is no timeline for healing—it is simply in God's time and in how you continue to process your pain—there is hope! Take a moment to reflect on your process of becoming untangled.

Which types of triggers (visual, auditory, olfactory, etc.) do you struggle with? Name two or three specific triggers that affect you most often. Why do you feel this is so?

_____

_____

In the list of trigger-coping techniques, which one or two will you try this week? How do you think these will help? Make sure to record them and keep track of how well they work, so you can see a pattern.

_____

_____

How will you know you are continuing to heal, untangle, and create your solid three-legged stool?

_____

_____

"The name of the LORD is a
fortified tower; the righteous run
to it and are safe."

— PROVERBS 18:10

"I lift up my eyes to the mountains—
where does my help come from?
My help comes from the LORD,
the Maker of heaven and earth."

— PSALM 121:1–2

"Heal me, LORD, and I will be healed; save me
and I will be saved, for you are the one I praise."

— JEREMIAH 17:14

PRAYER

*God, thank You that You are continuing to walk with
me on this healing journey. You are so faithful. You see
the hard places, the times I am triggered, the times when
my patience with myself has grown thin. Thank You that
you clearly see what I am healing from and provide the
means to continue to move forward, step by step, into a*

life that is free of past gunk! Thank You that You desire good for my life, and that even as I pray in this moment, You are helping me grow, change, and restore a life back to health.

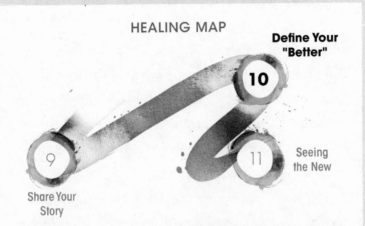

Chapter 11

HEALING OUT LOUD

Termination. *Michelle said not to take it personally, that's simply the official counseling term for the final session with a client. Today was the only time I've been terminated. And it felt pretty good. Like a hard-won promotion or a graduation. Who knew that an* ending *could feel so much like a* beginning?

This year of counseling was one of the most difficult seasons of my life. But I would do it again in an instant. It was the best investment I've ever made. One that has already been transformative in my life and my family in so many ways. I wish I had done it earlier. I hope I have opportunities to encourage other women to jump in the deep end too. The experience was nothing like I expected and everything that I needed.

Today, we spent some time talking about both the journey behind us and the one before me. I was in the exact same physical spot on the counseling couch that I've sat in for a year. But in so many ways, it feels like I have moved. Michelle reiterated some of the mile markers and victories. I couldn't stop smiling. It felt like every

tear that had been shed in that office was purposeful and
meaningful. Perhaps they watered something I didn't
even know was underground in my life. Something that
is budding anew. I pray and believe it will be beautiful.

— Sandi

During our final counseling session, Michelle and I talked about then-and-now markers from the journey. It felt completely different sitting on her couch that day than it did a year ago. Lighthearted. Secure. Joyful. In the same spot where I had previously felt broken. Defeated. Unwanted.

When I began the counseling journey, I didn't want anyone to know. Shame had convinced me that reaching out for help was an acknowledgement of failure. I didn't even tell my husband about the counseling sessions for months. As I think back on that decision, it seems so illogical and rooted in fear. It was a good reminder of who I was then and how far I had come.

In that small counseling room, there had been too many aha moments to count. Perhaps there were more to come? As we sat there reflecting on the journey, it hit me. From the first phone call to Michelle until now, I had been healing out loud. All along.

Every step was necessary. Showing up each week. Being honest. Putting words to pain. Processing. Grieving. Screaming. Surrendering. Battling. Having vulnerable conversations. Trusting. Forgiving.

It didn't always feel significant or like progress, but as I sat for the final time on that couch, I saw the journey from a different vantage point. I had been healing from the very first jump into the deep end. And thankfully, there's no termination to healing.

I thought back to our first discussion. The warning lights. Those loud indicators that something was off balance. I had talked into a microphone professionally for more than thirty years when I first entered Michelle's office. How ironic that I had never put words to the struggle before. This secret keeper was afraid to speak of past pain, shame, and the emotional turmoil within. Little did I know that "out loud" was such an important part of the healing process.

I think about every word spoken in that room, from both sides of the couch. The emotions expressed. The shame released. The hope shared. All out loud.

The hope carried. The peace found. The freedom discovered. All part of the healing journey.

Your pain and your journey may look very different from mine. But what I have found is that if there is something loud in your life (past pain, shame, guilt, unforgiveness, loss) there is also something powerful about saying it OUT LOUD. To yourself. To someone else (trusted friend or counselor). To God.

Processing out loud isn't a remedy or a fix, but it's helpful in a few ways. It validates your sense of loss; it brings the truth of the experience and the emotions connected to it together; and it's a "working out" that is good for the soul. A letting go.

A "declutching of the hands" around the pain. In doing so, my hands (and heart) were free to embrace healing more fully.

For me, the initial hesitation in sharing my wounds was fear of rejection. I was convinced that others would shame and reject me. But what I found to be true was the exact opposite. Michelle and my family offered comfort. Cried with me. Challenged the shame with me. And accepted me. I heard them. A gift that I wouldn't have received if I had not been willing to heal out loud.

I told Michelle that I still have the "imprints of shame" paper she gave me. I keep it in my journal. I can look at it now without crying. It's interesting. I still recognize those words (abuse, trauma, abandonment). They are still part of my story. But they don't define me any longer. It's like looking at a picture of a house I used to live in. It's familiar, but it isn't home. I've moved.

I asked Michelle what new imprints or markers she saw in my life. And would she write them down for me so I could keep both as a reminder of the work God is doing. After a brief moment of thought, she jotted down these words that I like to call my markers of change: joy, freedom, authentic relationships, healing.

I was right. God still had a few goose bumps for me during this last couch conversation. Seeing each word was meaningful and a reminder of the ongoing work of God in my life. Not hearing any loud rebuttals in my mind or heart was confirmation of change.

Michelle said it would be valuable for me to make my own

list as well. As I thought about it, the imprints of shame were words that described what had happened to me. The markers that I see now reflect what has been happening in me.

- *Truth teller.* I know the truth of who I really am. I'm no longer defined by past pain or shame. I know I am more than the sum of my past. I am treasured. Loved. Accepted.

- *Shame fighter.* I'm not tethered to past anger, fear, or self-protection. There's nothing hidden that is clamoring for my attention. I am free to be emotionally present and celebrate the good.

- *Street walker.* I'm allowing trusted people to know me fully. I enjoy not only giving love but having an ease and freedom in receiving love as well. More confidence in having vulnerable conversations. (Plus, the name always makes me smile.)

I'm hesitant to look at these markers as before and after because I don't think it honors the healing that is ongoing and still to come. Yucky moments and days still happen. But I feel more equipped to respond and not jump into a sinkhole of shame. I have learned tools, many of which we have shared in this book:

- Understanding emotional gauges or warning lights
- Discerning the difference between the voice of shame and the voice of truth
- Working through shame and ushering it out
- Grieving with hope

- Discovering a true identity
- Restoring relationships with ourselves, God, and others
- Battling for better

I look at every chapter written and point along the map as a tool in my healing toolbox. And honestly, hardly a day goes by that I don't use one or more of the tools. When shameful thoughts whisper and invite me to listen, I remind myself and my emotions of truth. Self-condemning thoughts do not monopolize the relationship or dialogue I have with myself. I pull out my Bible and my journal and remember who God is. Who I am. Where I've been. Where I'm going.

That newfound sense of security and healing flows out into every relationship I have. I treasure the ongoing vulnerable conversations with my husband, family, and trusted friends. And my circle of friends is growing. I'm not as fearful to say, "I would like to get to know you better," and allow others to know me better as well.

The sense of freedom I always hoped was possible is now an emerging reality in my mind and heart. And it impacts my life from every angle: personally, professionally, and spiritually. I feel restored. Not perfect. But, at peace with myself, my past, and my future. I'm learning to show grace to myself—because the journey and the battle continue.

About a year after I finished counseling, I had a disturbing dream. My husband actually woke me because I was whimpering, and he was concerned. My heart was pounding. I was afraid. And honestly, I didn't know if it was a dream or a flashback. All I knew for certain was that it felt like an emotional sucker punch. I was sad and frustrated. For days. I found myself wanting to emotionally withdraw. But I knew that wasn't healthy or productive.

After a few days, I reached out to Michelle and asked if we could talk. I shared about the dream and how it was affecting me. And in an effort to get every loud, raw emotion out, I said, "This feels like I'm right back where I was." With no hesitation, she said, "Sandi, you are not where you were. You aren't. Do you hear me? You are not where you were."

There were many other challenging and affirming words shared, but there was something sticky about her declaration. I wanted to believe that it was true. But I needed to get there in my own mind and heart as well. I prayed and asked God to quiet the loud voices of shame and reveal the truth. The picture He brought to my mind was me standing on a battlefield. I was still in the fight, but I was not in the same place I used to be. There had been victories small and large since then. Territory won. Movement made.

I realized I had interpreted the familiarity of the fight to mean that I was in the same place on the battleground. But that wasn't true. I was still fighting, but I was also moving forward. And do you know what that is called? Healing.

When you take the first step or continue to courageously share your feelings (out loud) . . . that is healing.

When others (including God) give you the gift of truth and you hear them, challenging your missteps . . . that is healing.

When you realize this is a marathon and not a sprint. But you continue to engage in the fight . . . that is healing.

The "ing" is important. Because it is the next step. The next good thing that God wants to do and is do-ing in your life.

Do you know that the first recorded good thing that God accomplished was done out loud? "And God *said*" (Genesis 1:3, emphasis mine). With those words, He began to speak all of creation into existence. Why words? Why not a snap of the finger? A wave of His hand? I don't know. That's for a theologian to address. But for reasons only He fully knows, He chose to speak out loud.

And then, before He was finished, He called it good. Each day. He looked at His incomplete work and said out loud, "It is good."

Can you dare to believe that God looks at you right now, incomplete and imperfect, and says, "Child, you are good, and I treasure you."

If that is beyond the reach of your mind and heart right now, that's okay. That's why Michelle and I wrote this book. To carry hope for you until you're able to carry it for yourself. To offer tools to help you journey on. A road map to help navigate through the loud, the pain, and the sorrow, and to celebrate the better. To encourage you to dig deep and embrace change. To believe the truth of God's design and love for you.

Your loud pain and healing path may look somewhat different from mine, but the starting point is the same. You start from wherever you are. Behind a chair, behind a microphone, behind imprints of shame. And you take the first step. You jump in and say, maybe for the first time, I don't want to be a secret keeper any longer. I want to be a shame fighter. A truth teller. A street walker. And you celebrate every mile marker in the healing journey.

As a recovering secret keeper, I had zero desire to write a book, share my yuck, and cross that busy street unclothed. But in time, God transformed my hesitancy into conviction. I saw it as yet another necessary, vulnerable conversation.

Within the pages of this book, I have let you into my bubble. At times it was uncomfortable for me. But I wanted you to know that I get it. I hear you. I understand the pain and the struggle with loving God while not liking yourself. My prayer is that you have connected with the vulnerability, understood the struggle, and will also share in the freedom and joy that I have found.

From personal experience and from the deep end of the pool, I can tell you that better and healing are possible. Joy comes in the morning. God is faithful. You are worth fighting for. Keep healing out loud, and I'll see you on the battlefield!

UNPACKING THE PROCESS
WITH DR. MICHELLE

Moving Toward the New

When you started this journey, your warning lights were blinking, and you may not have known exactly what that indicator light was telling you. Was it the shame indicator? Was it the pay-attention-to-your-emotion light? Was it the light showing that anger needed some attention? Or the one telling you that you needed to grieve and lament?

It might have been all of the above!

Everyone's struggles look different. Your story and your journey of healing are unique. How you have walked this path—through a paved, straight trail or a curving hike up and down the mountain—is a reflection of what God has for you.

Even though Sandi's story had similarities with others that I had heard in the counseling room, I could not have fully anticipated that it would turn out the way it did. I joke about the convenience of being able to read my clients' minds in session and to be able to predict the outcomes of therapy. (God has absolutely not given me this skill yet, and truthfully, I pray He never does!) We therapists hold tightly onto the hope that our clients will hear us and that they will be able to listen to themselves during this incredible opportunity to be challenged and to grow. Even my clients don't completely know the outcome of working through past pain and healing out loud in the therapy room.

But God knows. He knew the beginning, middle, and end of Sandi's story and her healing journey. He knows mine. And He knows yours too. Nothing is a surprise to God—nothing! Can we park for a moment in that kind of omniscience and even more so, His attentiveness to you? He has been with you during every step of your healing journey. Not just watching from a distance but coming up close to you as well. Directing you toward His truth. Speaking new words aloud to your hurting heart. Reminding you that you are not broken, but wounded. Challenging your shame-bound thoughts and feelings. Giving you freedom and confidence in Him. Forming you, gently, into this new shape. Amos 4:13 says, "He who forms the mountains, who creates the wind, and who reveals his thoughts to mankind, who turns dawn to darkness, and treads on the heights of the earth—the LORD God Almighty is his name."

This verse reveals the astounding work of a Creator God. He spoke the mountains into being. The power of the air is directed by Him. He turns light to dark, and dark to light. He sits in the highest of places here on Earth. And—don't miss this—He not only forms creation (and you) but also reveals Himself and His thoughts to us, we who are humble mankind. If He is who He is, and we are who He says we are, then we are beloved. Treasured. Convicted. Healing. Joyful. On a journey, not alone but with a renewed sense of His presence with us, helping us to see our shame and covering it with grace. Asking and receiving healing in the face of great pain. Helping us to shorten the distance between and bring Him and others close.

Remember, anything worth forming is also a process of patience. While Sandi's therapy process took a year, she noted that it is still ongoing. Yours will be too. The healing journey doesn't stop until we stand before Jesus, face-to-face, and receive His full gift of restoration.

We still live, of course, in a broken world that will trigger painful memories or thoughts, and we will struggle to react well to these triggers. You may feel that you're moving backward when this occurs, but that just means something needs to be revisited for additional healing. Repeat after me: it is not a failure to revisit some of our pain. The great news is God does not ask you to go places without Him. He does not ask you to revisit painful places without return. He promises to continue to bring you to places to see His truth, His conviction, and His love.

Remember the *kintsugi* process of breaking a jar and putting it back together with all of its pieces chipped, cracked, and scarred? We may try to present a perfect jar (at this point, we know that's both impossible and exhausting, right?), but that doesn't allow light to shine through the natural cracks and crevices. This process is not at all about throwing away the pieces, but carefully, deliberately, and patiently putting them back together to display again. Broken objects are not something to hide. Broken—or, in our cases, wounded—things are still beautiful. A jar put back together deserves to be seen.

I encourage you to consider a few things as you continue on your journey. First, consider holding a curiosity about your path forward. If God has brought you this far, how much more does He have for you? Yes, there will be trials and tribulations in the future. No doubt! However, when we can move forward without such a burden of past pain, it can free us up to be curious about what life will bring. Curiosity allows us to embrace the unfamiliar path and continue to learn what God has for us ahead.

Second, when you began this book, you were entering into it with some sort of hopefulness. Hope that you are not alone in your emotions. Hope that you were not alone in your thoughts. Hope that someone else could relate to your pain. Hope that you would stop reacting out of this pain. Hope that you would be able to deepen your relationship with God, with others, with yourself. As Alexander Pope wrote in *An Essay on Man*, "Hope springs eternal in the human breast." This is such an encouraging phrase! There is very little that can strip us of all of our hope. At the end of this part of your process, consider your own hope: is it springing anew? Are there places that are still dry, without much hope? If so, consider Hebrews 11:1: "Now faith is confidence in what we hope for and assurance about what we do not see." You may not see the end of your healing journey just yet, but take heart and hope, we can have the confidence to walk it through because of Jesus.

Third, don't miss the joy in your healing. Allow yourself to recognize the opportunity for great joy in the middle of your healing. Joy is the soul-deep assurance that helps us face the pain and the knowledge that God is carrying us through it. You may feel a defiant kind of joy, after battling your way through. You may feel a contented kind of joy as you are spending more time with God. You may feel a bubble-up kind of joy as you rest in God's promises and love for you. Joy doubles down on the sense of purpose, hope, and fruit of all the work that you have done and God has done through you so far. Know that while you are still a work in progress, pain and joy can reside together. That's the power of "and"—both parts can be simultaneously true. We can grieve and be glad. We can be imperfect and loved. We can be accepted and vulnerable. We can be wounded and healing.

So what are your next steps as you journey on?

- *Pray.* Say a prayer of surrender to God. Give Him your life. Your pain and struggle. Ask Him to reveal Himself and His love to you. His Word is full of truth and hope. Spend time each day in it. The psalms are a good place to start.

- *Reach out.* Find someone you trust to journey with you. A counselor. A friend. Share your feelings with them and allow them to speak truth to you lovingly. In time, you may also want to invite someone else to jump in.

- *Journal.* Write scriptures that speak to you. Write your honest thoughts and prayers. It can be difficult to see change day to day. But a journal helps you see the mile markers along the way and how you've seen God work in your life.

- *Read this book again.* Early in our counseling journey, Michelle asked me to read a book she thought
  would be helpful: *The Wounded Heart* by Dan
  Allender. It's a powerful book about healing from
  abuse. The first time I read it as fast as I could. I felt
  shame and anxiety with every page. I kept looking
  for the chapter with the fix, and it never came. She
  asked me to read it again. After an extended eye roll,
  I leaned in and read it again. The second reading was
  so much more helpful. There was less pressure and
  anxiety, and I gleaned so much more insight.

- *Read the epilogue.* It's one more vulnerable conversation we get to have together.

REFLECTION

You've been on your own healing journey, following your path as God has led you. Take a moment to consider how far you have come in your story with the reflection questions and exercises below.

What are your markers of progress?

_____

_____

Take a moment to return to your own "triangle" place of shame or dislike or rejection (found in chapter two). What did it look like? Take a moment to fill in your own triangle below as a reminder:

Now, consider your healing process as you have read this book. God may have brought certain words to mind: loved, valued, seen, whichever! Use the four-pointed graphic below to fill in the words. (Why we are using a kite graphic will become clear in the epilogue!) What words do you use to describe yourself and the outcome of all of your incredible work?

What does your next step look like as you finish reading this book? For example, you may take up the challenge to heal out loud with a friend, a family member, or a counselor. You may decide to share this book with someone who needs it, or you may use the resources in the back of the book to continue your healing process.

_____

_____

SCRIPTURE

"But those who hope in the LORD
will renew their strength.
They will soar on wings like eagles;
they will run and not grow weary,
they will walk and not be faint."

— ISAIAH 40:31

"Then Nehemiah the governor, Ezra the priest
and teacher of the Law, and the Levites who were
instructing the people said to them all, 'This day
is holy to the LORD your God. Do not mourn or
weep.' For all the people had been weeping as
they listened to the words of the Law. Nehemiah
said, 'Go and enjoy choice food and sweet
drinks, and send some to those who have nothing
prepared. This day is holy to our Lord. Do not
grieve, for the joy of the LORD is your strength.'"

— NEHEMIAH 8:9–10

"You turned my wailing into dancing; you
removed my sackcloth and clothed me with joy,
that my heart may sing your praises
and not be silent."

— Psalm 30:11-12

PRAYER

*God, I bring myself to You—my whole self, all the
wounded, shameful, hurt pieces of my past and present. I
haven't always considered myself Your beautiful creation,
Your beloved, Your treasured. But I declare today that
I am free, that I am comforted, and that I am strong
because You say I am! Help me see this, Lord, even
when it seems that my situation and relationships say
otherwise. Thank You that You are doing a good work in
me. You are helping me untangle my knottiest of places
so I can be free in You and so I can tell others of Your
freedom. I'm resting in that truth today.*

EPILOGUE

SANDI

During my senior year in high school, my boyfriend (now husband) and I broke up. In an effort to process my feelings, I put pen to paper. I wasn't yet ready to tell my story to anyone else, but unknowingly, I did begin to write it. No one ever read it, but it served a purpose for me. It was the first time any of my inner stuff made its way out, in any form. But once on paper, it sat. For decades. In fact, I forgot about it until I was in counseling.

I dug it out of storage and, while reading it, realized there was now more of the story to write. Much more. So, I did. Below is the complete story from the pen of a seventeen-year-old, followed with the rest of my life to date. My hope in including it here is that it resonates with you and reminds you of the future and freedom God is authoring for you.

The Kite

There once was a kite that loved to fly. But she felt different. She wasn't colorful or pretty or graceful like the other kites. She was plain. And awkward. And a bit rough around her kite edges. She didn't know why. She simply knew what she knew—that she was not a very good kite.

She even questioned why God made her a kite if she couldn't be a good one. Kites are supposed to be graceful and bring joy to those around them. How could this kite do that? She couldn't. She knew it. And she was sad.

One day the kite was flying with her dad. She was in the sky, and he was standing on the ground holding the string. She loved him and was thankful that he was holding onto her. She smiled. But as she was playfully moving across the sky, she looked down into his eyes. She didn't see pride. Or love. Or anything beautiful.

Apparently, he didn't see anything beautiful either because he let go of the string. He let her go. And he walked away.

The kite was confused and sad. She was afraid. She felt rejected. The kite cried because of what her father had done. And the kite crashed to the ground, tattered and torn.

The kite flew again. She was still sad and scared, but flying is what kites do. After a while, the kite felt a tug. She looked down and noticed a stranger holding on to the string. He was demanding. He tugged and pulled to control the kite. The kite tried to pull free, but he won the fight. She lost the fight.

She lost a lot.

And then the man let go of the string. And he walked away. The kite crashed to the ground more tattered and torn.

Eventually, the kite returned to the sky. But flying was different now. Day by day, the kite flew with her string a little longer. It felt safer that way. If no one saw her, no one could hurt her.

But one day, the kite noticed a young man looking her way. She saw that his eyes were kind and curious. He smiled. He asked if he could fly the kite. She said yes and felt his strong but gentle hands take hold of the string.

It was like nothing the kite had experienced before. He was gentle and thoughtful. He told the kite that she was beautiful. The kite didn't want to believe him, but she saw something in his eyes that she had never seen before. It was wonderful. She smiled.

The young man said he loved the kite. She loved him too. She was, for once, feeling free to dance. So, she did. Then, without warning, he let go of the string. And he walked away.

The kite was devastated. Betrayed. Again. The kite cried because love always hurts. The kite crashed to the ground more tattered and torn.

One day, the kite noticed something was wrong. She could still feel the breeze. She could see the sky above and the ground below. But that was the problem—she saw the same piece of sky and the same piece of ground. She was stuck, tangled in the trees. How long had she not noticed?

The kite did everything she knew to get free. But the more she struggled, the more tangled she got. It seemed impossible. And so unfair.

And then it occurred to her that she hadn't gotten tangled by herself, and she probably wouldn't get free by herself either. In desperation, the kite cried out for help. Almost in reply, the breeze picked up. The presence of the wind was strong and reassuring. The kite hoped that the force of the breeze alone would help her quickly shake free. She believed it could. But it seemed as though the wind had another plan. It was as if the breeze was forcefully, intentionally blowing on only one tangle at a time. As it blew, the kite shook. It felt unsettling, like she was losing her grip. But wasn't that what she wanted?

The kite realized that with each untangled string came a new sense of release. Shame . . . Rejection . . . Hurt . . . Pain . . . One by one the knots and tangles were exposed and freed. It was painful. But the pain had purpose. With each gust of wind, another tree limb let go of the kite. Or was the kite letting go? Either way, freedom was coming. Piece by piece. Peace. She smiled.

Freedom felt different than she'd thought it would. She was still tattered and torn. But the intrusive branches weren't in her way any longer. She had experienced them. Learned from them. And was now flying past them. Resolved. Lighter. Content.

Occasionally, the branches would call out to the kite with an enticing, familiar voice. But every time the kite heard the invitation, she also heard the breeze. It, too, was calling. The kite had a renewed passion to fly. And instead of feeling different, ugly, or bad, the kite felt treasured. Free. She wanted to dance again. So, she did. And she smiled.

The more the kite flew, the more she noticed something. From a distance, every kite looked beautiful. And yet the closer she got to them, the more she realized they were tattered and torn too. It didn't diminish their beauty. It simply spoke of their struggles and stories. So many tattered and torn kites.

The kite also saw some of the other kites were still tangled in the trees. They hadn't discovered freedom. Yet. But what if . . . ?

What if this was part of the kite's purpose? Every kite's purpose? To experience the breeze, learn to dance, and help other kites find freedom? What if the more tattered and torn you were, the more hope you could share? What if every time a tattered and torn kite danced in the sky, it pointed to something undeniable? Something beautiful?

That made the kite want to dance. So, she did. And He smiled.

"He brought me out into a spacious place; he rescued me because he delighted in me."

— Psalm 18:19

ACKNOWLEDGMENTS

MICHELLE

To the One who created this book in the first place: Abba Father. Thank You for inviting me to tell part of Your story to our readers. You are the author of all stories, and I dedicate this work to You above all. My prayer has always been that we have honored and glorified You through the words on these pages.

To my husband, Jason, for your unwavering support of all my crazy ideas and dreams. Not only a cheering section, but one who loves me for me as well. What a gift you are. "My beloved is mine and I am his" (Song of Songs 2:16).

Thank you to my girlfriends for responding when I texted you, "What do you think about this title?" and "Do you really think I can do this?" Your responses were quick and sweetly reassuring and thoughtful. You model Jesus to me each day.

To Sandi: my unexpected friend! Not only are you my coauthor, but also a treasured friend. True. Steady. Honest. Loving. All that and a bag of gummy worms!

To Dexterity, all the amazing staff, and our wing-woman and editor, Leslie Peterson: You saw what two shiny, brand-new authors were trying to do, and encouraged us with a perfect balance of honesty, optimism, and wisdom. You have helped make this book beyond what we could have dreamed. Thank you.

SANDI

To my heavenly Father, who loved me before I was aware. Who redeemed my life. And continues to heal and restore the wounded places. Your faithfulness and grace have changed my life and my family. Thank You for rewriting our story. It is for Your glory that we share it out loud.

To Mike: you are patient, kind, and rock-solid. You know me best and love me still. You are my one. Forever. I thank God for you and the life we have. Thank you for fighting for us. I love you.

To Danelle, Nathan, Miguel, Kirk, and Lexie: you are God's richest blessings in my life. In God's good providence He made us a family. The depth of love and friendship is rare and rich. I love you.

To Michelle: you had a front-row seat to the healing journey. For that, and for you, I am forever grateful. Thank you for saying, "Yes." To friendship, to sharing the story, and to flying pigs. All things are possible, my friend!

To our editor, Leslie Peterson, and Matt West, our publisher at Dexterity: Thank you for believing in us and helping us shape and share the story. I'm thankful for your confidence, wisdom, and friendship.

FURTHER READING

Allender, Dan. 2008. *Wounded Heart: Hope for Adult Victims of Childhood Sexual Abuse.* **Colorado Springs: NavPress.**

An intensely personal and compassionate look at the effects—and hope of healing—from sexual abuse. This book goes beyond the general issues and solutions suggested in other books.

Allender, Dan. 2016. *Healing the Wounded Heart: The Heartache of Sexual Abuse and the Hope of Transformation.* **Grand Rapids: Baker Books.**

For the millions who have suffered abuse in the forms of rape, incest, molestation, sexting, sexual bullying, pornography, and more, hope doesn't come easily—but Allender helps to light the way to renewed joy, one step at a time.

Benner, David. 2015. *The Gift of Being Yourself: The Sacred Call to Self-Discovery.* **Downers Grove: IVP Books.**

Discerning your true self is inextricably related to discerning God's purposes for you. Paradoxically, the more you become like Christ, the more you become authentically yourself. In this exploration of Christian identity, psychologist and spiritual director David G. Benner illuminates the spirituality of self-discovery.

Brown, Brené. 2012. *Daring Greatly: How the Courage to Be Vulnerable Transforms the Way We Live, Love, Parent, and Lead.* **New York: Avery.**

Vulnerability is the core of difficult emotions like grief, fear, and disappointment, but also the birthplace of love, belonging, joy, empathy, innovation, and creativity. This book is about courage—the courage to "step into the arena" of relationships and life.

Brown, Sandi. 2021. *A Little More Peace: 100 Devotions to Help Settle Your Soul.* **St. Louis: JoyFM.**

This is Sandi's most recent devotional, and it is easy to take to heart . . . even an anxious one. A perfect way to start your day, hear from God, and find a little more peace.

Buechner, Frederick. 1991. *Telling Secrets.*
San Francisco: Harper.

A moving autobiography about the destructive power of a child-hood secret and how the telling of that secret has brought the author healing, hope, and a graceful experience of love.

Cloud, Henry, and John Townsend. 2017. *Boundaries: When to Say Yes, How to Say No to Take Control of Your Life.* **Grand Rapids: Zondervan.**

People often focus so much on being loving and giving that they forget their own limits. "No" is probably one of the most difficult words in the English language, and this guide provides biblically based answers to setting healthy boundaries.

James, John W., and Russell Friedman. 2009. *The Grief Recovery Handbook: The Action Program for Moving Beyond Death, Divorce, and Other Losses including Health, Career and Faith.* **New York: HarperCollins.**

There are many valid losses in addition to the death of a loved one. When the grief process is incomplete, it can have lifelong negative effects on the capacity for happiness and peace. This book offers grievers specific actions needed to move through loss toward integration.

Muller, Wayne. 1993. *Legacy of the Heart: The Spiritual Advantages of a Painful Childhood.* New York: Touchstone.

In this book, Muller gives readers a path to heal from past trauma, which might include physical or sexual abuse, loss, or alcoholism.

Powlison, David. 2016. *Good and Angry: Redeeming Anger, Irritation, Complaining, and Bitterness.* Greensboro: New Growth Press.

An exploration of God's anger and ours. This book is chock-full of practical help for all who struggle with how to respond when life sparks anger. It answers the question: how can we express anger in a way that is both faithful and fruitful?

Thompson, Curt. 2015. *The Soul of Shame: Retelling the Stories We Believe About Ourselves.* Downers Grove: InterVarsity Press.

Whether we see it or not, shame affects every aspect of our personal and professional lives. It seeks to destroy our identity in Jesus Christ. This book includes theological and practical tools necessary to identify shame and dismantle it.

Van der Kolk, Bessel. 2014. *The Body Keeps the Score: Brain, Mind, and Body in the Healing of Trauma.* New York: Viking.

In this book, author and researcher van der Kolk transforms our understanding of traumatic stress, revealing how it literally rearranges the brain's wiring—specifically areas dedicated to pleasure, engagement, control, and trust.

Vroegop, Mark. 2019. *Dark Clouds, Deep Mercy: Discovering the Grace of Lament.* **Wheaton: Crossway.**

Lament is how you live between the poles of a hard life and trusting God's goodness. This book invites readers to grieve, struggle, and tap into the rich reservoir of grace and mercy that God offers in the darkest moments of life.

Young, Sarah. 2004. *Jesus Calling: Enjoying Peace in His Presence.* **Nashville: Thomas Nelson.**

Spend time with Jesus through this book, and find reassurance, comfort, and gentle guidance. This book will take you on a yearlong journey of connection with Jesus through reflection and meditation based on God's Word.

WEB RESOURCES

GoodTherapy: Find the right therapist

www.goodtherapy.org

Faithful Counseling: Professional mental health counseling from a biblical perspective

www.faithfulcounseling.com

Mental Health America: Advocacy and education

www.mhanational.org

National Alliance on Mental Illness: Advocacy, group directory, local resources

www.nami.org

Psychology Today: Therapist directory

www.psychologytoday.com/us/therapists

ABOUT THE AUTHORS

Sandi Brown is a radio personality, author, and respected leader of two successful radio stations in St. Louis, Missouri: Joy FM and BOOST RADIO, which have a combined reach of more than five hundred thousand people each week. She is the founder and president of Gateway Creative Broadcasting and a chairperson for Christian Music Broadcasters. Sandi is a graduate of Maryville University, where she studied communications and marketing. She lives with her husband, Mike, in Columbia, Illinois. *Healing Out Loud* is her third book.

Dr. Michelle Caulk, licensed professional counselor, has worked through counseling private practices and ministries to help bring Jesus's hope and healing to the most challenging times of life, including grief and trauma. Michelle is a graduate of Southern Illinois University at Edwardsville with a bachelor of arts in English literature, the University of Illinois with a master of science in library and information science, and Argosy University with a master of arts in mental health counseling. Michelle also obtained her doctorate of philosophy in counselor education and supervision and is an assistant professor and director of clinical experiences at Huntington University in Indiana. *Healing Out Loud* is her first book—not counting her dissertation!